I0092892

DIVINING
GUIDANCE

TALES FROM A LIFE OF
DOWSING & INSIGHT

BILL NORTHERN
with Cesca Janece Waterfield

ALSO BY BILL NORTHERN

That Yank With the Crystal

HONEY HOUSE

PRESS + BOOK HIVE

DIVINING
GUIDANCE

TALES FROM A LIFE OF
DOWSING & INSIGHT

Divining Guidance: Tales from a Life of Dowsing & Insight
© 2022 Bill Northern

ISBN 979-8-9858733-0-6

ISBN e-book 979-8-9858733-1-3

Library of Congress Control Number: 2022933935

All rights reserved. No part of this book may be reproduced without permission in writing from the publisher, Honey House Hive at info@honeyhousehive.com. Visit us at honeyhousehive.com.

Cover photo provided courtesy of the author.
Cover design by Cesca Janece Waterfield.

Printed in the United States of America

Table of Contents

Good Friends Are Good for Business

My Angels, Dowsing & Communication

The Healing Journals

Further Insight

Bill's Acknowledgments

I am writing this book to encourage all dowsers that they are able to all things with dowsing and GOD. Stacy Boyd. Aliyah Nichols, Kyle Ogle, Annie Robinson helped with typing the first drafts many years ago, as Gail St. Denis did with the story on Bettie.

Thanks to The American Society of Dowsers and Dick Paskowski for teaching me to dowse. Dowsing completely changed my life. Dowsing in essence helps one to listen more carefully to God, or as I say, to my Angels. God is probably too busy to listen to all my questions. So my Angels tell me what God wants us to know and do.

I want to thank again the lady who brought in two horses for us to dowse on first day of dowsing school in 1994. I want to also thank Mark Leone for being the first person with jumping horses to use us and tell others about how beneficial our readings were to him and his crew. Thanks to Kim Jungherr for being one of the first Hunter division riders to use us and tell others.

Hugo Merry was the first to bring us to Ireland to read and teach. He told the folks at Coolmore about us which resulted in more visits to Ireland and some stories still being told there.

I had been doing a lot of remote readings for John Hayes who talked me into shifting to Lexington, Kentucky, from Warsaw, Virginia.

My thanks to Alice Tse who has among other titles, Chair of the Nursing Department at the University of Hawaii. Alice was one of my best students. A good friend of hers had been in the hospital over three weeks, and not getting any better. So Alice and I dowsed each of her 22 medications. We eliminated all but six. Alice went to her head doctor and explained what we did. He ordered that all but those six be stopped. She left the hospital a short time after that. Alice had two Yorkies and taught me that animals were like children. They appreciated anything you brought them when you had been away awhile. A handful of peas from a restaurant meal made them quite happy.

I would be terribly remiss if I failed to mention my friend Tyrone Burrowes in Rakaia, New Zealand. Tyrone has a large house and always makes his house available for me to give dowsing lessons. He is also my web master responsible for my web site. When I give him advice he says, "Yeah, yeah.," and then does exactly what he was going to do anyway.

Finally, I had been trying to have my book published for years but kept having problems. People just couldn't believe what we do. Then along came Cesca Waterfield. She just took an interest in the book and I gave her my stories. Shortly, she had my book ready. If you want a book published, call Cesca.

Bill Northern, Florida
February 2022

Cesca's Acknowledgments

Many people helped enrich the development and writing of this book. I'm grateful to Ren and Alison Ellett, President and Editor respectively, of The New Zealand Society of Dowsing and Radionics. They worked around time differences in New Zealand and the U.S. to speak with me. My thanks to Gladys McCoy of The Ozark Research Institute in Fayetteville, Arkansas, who took time to talk about her late husband, founder of The Institute, Harold McCoy.

I wish to thank Michael Leahy of Florida and Ireland, who recounted his experiences as a horse stable manager and bloodstock consultant who worked with Bill.

Fleet Dillard III and Billy Herbert of Virginia both took time to share stories about friendship and work with Bill. David Jett of The Richmond County Museum and The Essex County Museum in Virginia, kindly opened up Museum photo archives. Thanks also to Leroy Troxell at The Virginia Horse Center Foundation in Lexington, Virginia.

Beta readers gave their time and insight, including Debbie Filipkowski O'Keefe, Randall Williams, and Victor Fredette III.

I want to extend my gratitude to John Crehan for his time and photo expertise. I must also thank John Dessen of Illini Studio of Illinois for photo assistance and inspiration.

At last, my love and heartfelt thanks to my husband Randy Helchen for believing in and supporting me.

Cesca Janece Waterfield Helchen
July 2022

Foreword

DIVINING GUIDANCE

An Invitation to Believe

By Fleet Dillard III

Sudie was a millennial dog. Born December 27, 1999, she was dark yellow in color and heavy-boned, even for a Lab. Like most of my dogs, she came to be known affectionately as "Pig." In the fall of 2000, I was fishing for striper alone in the Rappahannock River. My neighbor and wife arrived by boat and they had "the look" about them. I knew someone was dead or seriously injured. They explained there had been an accident involving Sudie and a golf cart driven by one of my neighbor's children. We rushed up the river, looked at Sudie, and determined she had broken her back. Through the generosity and friendship that we shared, my neighbor, an orthopedic surgeon, offered a "blank check" to fix the injury. At a clinic in Northern Virginia, Sudie had a pin placed through her last vertebrae. She was young and recovered quickly – in about eight weeks.

But nine years later, Sudie's tail seemed to hurt her. For years Sudie had been active retrieving upland birds and waterfowl, and jumping off docks. But now, she winced if you pinched her tail in an effort to find the source of her pain. I assumed the old injury was rearing up. So I took her to the veterinarian. Many questions were asked, but I left with the old "Take two aspirin and call me in the morning" routine. I dropped Sudie off at the house and walked down the street to get lunch. That's when I ran into Bill. He had parked his Ford on Prince Street in Tappahannock to eat at Rivahside Café where we often had lunch. He's from the Northern Neck and would come over to Tappahannock to catch up on politics, the economy, and people in general.

Bill greeted me with those angelic blue eyes that always look like they might shed a tear. The unmistakable hat, a smile on his face, and a gentle voice that carries out the last syllables softly. I told him about my morning and about my dog's pain in her tail. Bill knew nothing of her past injury and I did not mention it. He asked the dog's name. As we stood in the 90-degree sun on the sidewalk, Bill closed his eyes, lowered his head, and said nothing. Forty-five seconds went by and he looked up with a slight smile. "We are not sensing anything in the tail. Rather it seems to be the last vertebrae."

I laughed and told him about the injury and the pin from years ago. "Where is Sudie?" he asked. I told him she was at the house some four blocks away. Bill suggested that we ride down the street to see her. I got in the passenger seat and looked behind me to stare at the white letters on the back window of Bill's Ford that read, *Animal Communicator.* We arrived, and I let Sudie out to see him. Notwithstanding her pain, she moved fairly well and approached Bill who was kneeling down to greet her. She licked her lips and then spun around to lean on him. Bill pulled out one of those rubber change holders you used to get at the barber shop. He squeezed it and out came a brass plumb bob about the length of the last knuckle on your pinky finger. It was connected to a purple string. He placed it between his ring and middle finger and set the plumb in motion: *Left, right, left, right,* while he ran his other hand along Sudie's back. He started at her shoulders while I watched carefully. When he reached the last vertebrae, the plumb started to spin counterclockwise. He moved from that spot, and the plumb resumed, *left, right.* He repeated this three times and the plumb did the same thing. But to my eye, Bill's hand holding the string connected to the plumb never moved. He stood up and gave me a plan of action. He attributed his instructions to his knowledge from working with horses in Australia and New Zealand as well as his time in Kentucky counseling veterinarians, horse owners, and jockeys. He said, "Fleet, go get some pure aloe and vanilla yogurt. Rub the aloe deeply into her skin at the vertebrae. Get it through the fur. Feed her yogurt."

I heeded his advice. Two days later, Sudie was jumping in the back of the truck, running, and acting like she was fine – and she was, until two years later when she first went blind, and later deaf. As her other senses declined, her nose became even better and she was able to dove-hunt throughout all of this. I let her out every night and she always returned.

Then one night she did not come back. My wife and I went looking for her separately and communicated by phone. I felt it was not going to end well. So I called Bill. After I told him of the situation, he said he would call me back. A few minutes later, my phone rang. Bill said, "We're sensing tombstones, a graveyard." My heart sank.

But then my phone beeped with an incoming call. "I found Sudie!" my wife exclaimed. "In the cemetery of St. John's Church, just walking around sniffing the ground." Even though she couldn't see, Sudie was like the proverbial blind pig with heightened smell who found an acorn. I jumped back on the phone with Bill, elated. Sudie went on to live a happy two more years.

My wife never put any credence in Bill's stories. She is not unlike many who have difficulty imagining the "communication" with animals and angels.

Angels? Yeah, that's right. That's the reason Bill often speaks in the first person plural when he is working. "We all have angels, Fleet," he once told me. "You just have to learn how to communicate with them."

Like many all over the world who have provided stories about Bill, you can believe.

Tappahannock, Virginia
July 1, 2022

Colt Follies

Young Bill Northern stands in front of his father's business, Warsaw Department Store.

The Future Salesman & Budding Communicator

I was born in a small two-bedroom house on Hamilton Boulevard in Warsaw, Virginia. Warsaw is a small town even today. But back then, it was tiny! My bedroom was in the front of the house facing the road. One night in 1943, I woke up to a commotion going on outside my window and it frightened me. I was only five years old. This was during World War II, and everything was rationed. It was tough times for everybody. I went into my Daddy's bedroom and woke him up. He and I came back to my window and looked outside. There were two men taking the tires off my father's car. He recognized them.

"I'm just going to let them have the tires, Billy," he told me.

"But why, Daddy?"

"They need tires to go to work," he said. "But as you know, I can walk to work."

Early Lessons in Business

Saturday was a big deal in Warsaw. Everyone came to town and I got to work in my Daddy's store. Early on, my father had worked for a couple of "dry goods" stores in town. One was Dunaway's and the other was Miller's. But he had decided to open up his own store and name it Warsaw Department Store. It was there he taught me how to make change. Even before I started school, I could give change for a 20 dollar bill. Those bills were rare back then. I was usually in charge of the Toy Department and sometimes I got to buy a toy. My Daddy said, "You can buy what you want, but you've also got to sell them." I wasn't very good at selling girl toys like dolls, but I was good at selling baseballs, puzzles, and things I knew boys liked to play with.

The Day My Chaps Caught Fire

I was obsessed with anything pertaining to horses and

cowboys – imagine that! – and my father loved to spoil me. One day he gave me a pair of chaps. They weren't just regular chaps, these were fuzzy chaps. I already had on my cowboy shirt and I had my play guns, so of course, I put on my new fuzzy chaps. Back then, everyone burned their trash, so there were always embers leftover from a fire the night before for me to play around in. On this particular morning, I was fooling around in the embers and all of a sudden my fuzzy chaps shot up into flames. I don't remember who it was, but someone came over and rolled me around on the ground to put the fire out. They probably saved my life. Needless to say, I was burned badly on both legs. My burns were so bad that I was in bed for two and a half months. Back in those days, they would put butter on burns. My mother and her friends like Barbara Walker took turns a few times a day to rub butter all over my legs.

*Bill's father, James Alvin Northern, holds young
Bill alongside his beloved birddog, Boots.*

My Father & His Birddog, Boots

When I was young, my Daddy, James Alvin Northern, had a birddog named Boots. Daddy taught me how to shoot a gun safely and bird hunt with Boots at a very young age. On Sunday mornings, Daddy would listen to gospel music on the radio. I can remember laying my head down on Boots by the wood stove. After gospel hour, we listened to the reading of the comic strips. Some people didn't get a newspaper, including us, so a guy would come on the radio and read them to everyone, comics like Little Orphan Annie, Gasoline Alley, and Blondie.

At Daddy's store, I remember there were customers that would come in and not have any money to pay for what they needed. He would always let them "put it on a ticket" so they could pay him back when they could, like a charge account. I never saw him turn anyone down if they needed something and could not pay for it. Even if you owed him money for months, if you needed something, he would still let you have it. I noticed at a young age that there were some people that took advantage of my father's generosity by making him feel sorry for them. I can recall when back-to-school time would roll around and all the kids would need one important thing: new shoes. We went barefoot all summer! But as school approached, parents would bring their children into the store to get new shoes. If the parents didn't have the money to pay for the shoes, it was okay. My father would let them put the shoes on a ticket.

My Daddy's homeplace was around seven miles away from the store in an area called Folly Neck which is close to a little area called Emmerton. Back then, many people of color had to walk to church on Sunday mornings because many didn't own a vehicle or a horse and buggy. Many folks later told me that if my Daddy saw them walking to church and he was driving, he would tell them to get in. He'd give them a ride and give them a little money to put into the offering plate.

In 1945, when I was just a young fella, my father left for Baltimore, Maryland, to go on a buying trip and never returned. He passed away on the trip. I was only seven years old. After that, I always felt he was trying to contact me and I tried to contact him. That's when I started to teach myself magic. I thought practicing magic would allow me to somehow communicate with my father.

After Daddy died, my mother was shocked at the thousands of dollars that customers owed to him. We had to move upstairs over the store to save money. In winter, we had an old wood stove, no oil stove until I was around 12. We had a very little back yard where we stored wood. It was my job to take the wood up the stairs. All I could put in my arms is what I could take upstairs at a time. It took several trips to haul all of wood.

Next door was The Estes Trucking Company. The men would let me come over. I thought I was helping them, but I'm sure I wasn't. Sometimes if I threw my ball on our roof at home, it would break our asbestos shingles, so the men at Estes let me throw the ball up against their building.

My mother often took me to visit our family in Emmerton. As a treat, she would let me take Boots with us so that he and I could bird hunt while she visited with grandmother.

Olden Days in the Northern Neck

Like my father, my grandfather had died at an early age also. So at this time, my grandmother Lilly lived with her second husband in Emmerton. They didn't have running water or electricity, which meant you had to use the bathroom in the outhouse. At night, instead of venturing outside, we used what was called a "slop jar," which was a large bucket-shaped container that had rounded edges so that you could sit on it. First thing the next morning, the woman of the house usually had the wonderful job of taking the slop jar to the outhouse for disposal of its contents. No electricity meant that if you wanted to listen to a radio, you had to have one that was battery operated. I remember purchasing a large battery for the radio and it cost a pretty penny, but lasted a long time!

If you needed to see at night, light was provided by oil lamps. There was one oil lamp in particular that hung from the ceiling like a chandelier that lit up the whole room, like a light bulb, but not as bright.

My grandparents had a large wood stove. There were two sides to the stove top and my grandmother usually only used one side. If she was using the other side, that meant she was baking something, such as homemade bread.

I recall my grandmother smoking cigarettes. Even though they were available to purchase, she preferred to roll her own.

On their farm, there were geese, ducks, chickens, pigs, and cows. It was an entirely different world down at their house, much different than where we lived in the village of Warsaw, which had not yet been officially incorporated into a town. Life seemed much harder for my grandparents than it was for us in town. We had the convenience of having stores nearby. The biggest difference was that we had electricity at our house and they didn't. When I was a teenager, my grandparents finally got electricity. My grandmother refused to give up her wood stove for cooking though. She didn't want anything to do with a modern stove and insisted on using oil lamps for light because electricity was "too expensive."

Back in those days, there was a lot more togetherness. Families came together to help one another, whether it was a farmer that owned a tractor plowing a field for a friend who didn't own one, or herding escaped cows for a neighbor. Now it seems as though everyone wants to do their own thing and be independent of others.

Speaking of togetherness, hog-killing time was a very big deal back in those days and required families helping each other. Preparations usually began right after Thanksgiving when the temperatures started to drop. This went straight on through the month of January. I remember each family going from farm to farm to help one another with the process and it was an all-day affair. First, the women had to pull many buckets of water from the well, heat it to boiling on the wood stove while the men were doing the killing. The process usually involved a rifle and one bullet to the hog's head.

Then, onto the process of draining, boiling, separating and preparing the meat for storage. In exchange for helping each other, you received part of the hog. For instance, one person may have wanted the feet, and another the organs. The meat was stored by hanging it from the ceiling in what we called a smokehouse. Traditionally, a smokehouse was a small enclosed outbuilding with a vent, a single entrance, no windows, and it frequently had a pyramid-style roof. There was a firebox towards the back that contained natural hickory wood that would smolder and create smoke. The smokehouse served both as a meat smoker and a way to store the meats. Preservation occurred by salt curing and extended cold smoking for two weeks or longer. Smokehouses were always secured to prevent animals and thieves from accessing the food. The hams that were properly smoked and salted back then were very desirable. Today, there are few smokehouses around, but one that comes to mind is Edwards Virginia Smokehouse in Surry, Virginia.

I often think about how the good ol' days were. People seemed to enjoy their lives more back then, even though they didn't have the modern conveniences we do now. Everything moved at a slower pace and family was more important than it seems today.

A band director from Warsaw schools took students monthly to perform on a television show broadcast from Richmond. Bill is at the center.

The Young Magician

When my father died, I felt sure there was some way to contact him. I was just in second grade but I could read and I really wanted to contact him. I got books from everywhere on magic.

At that time, a TV station in Richmond, Channel 6, I believe it was, was using local kids to perform their talents on a show that aired before The Howdy Doody Show came on. Most people played instruments, so our band director took some students to Richmond for this. About once a month, I would go too and do a magic trick for the televised show. I had this box and after showing everybody it was empty, I would pull different things out of it. A rabbit or two dozen scarves! I had magic wands I'd throw in the air to catch things.

Performing on TV lasted right long, almost a year.

Many years later when my mom died, I found a report card that said, "Billy would be a good student if he would stop doing magic."

Leading the Lunchroom Strike

My mother always made me buy school lunches. But when I was in the third grade, school lunches were terrible. I can remember them serving us vegetable soup and I only counted two to three tiny vegetables in it. The meatloaf was mostly bread, and the hot dogs were mostly water. You could take one bite and the bun was soggy.

We were living above my father's store right in town. One day, just for the heck of it, I walked up to the A&P grocery store on my way to school, and got a can of pork and beans. I had swiped two pieces of bread from home, and put a can opener in my sack. When lunchtime came around, I pulled out my beans and bread. A lot of my classmates thought it was a good idea. So the next day I brought four cans of beans and a loaf of bread. My class loved it! My beans and bread tasted a whole lot better than the school lunches. The idea took off!

The next day, a high school student took me up to the store and we got a whole case of beans and a few loaves of bread. Gone! We only charged enough to pay for our expenses. By the end of the week, I brought in a couple loads of beans and bread, with a little help, of course, and extra can openers. All the kids loved it. There were maybe four students out of the entire school that still bought school lunch.

One lunchtime the next week, our principal, Mr. Hodges was standing in the back of the cafeteria. He was wearing his usual black suit, white shirt, and black tie. He was tall, and though he was balding up front, he had a spray of dark hair at the back of his head that stuck up like feathers. He yelled, "Mr. Bill Northern!" I pretended not to hear him.

"Mr. Bill Northern!" Hodges yelled again. I dragged my feet and stood before him.

"Do you have any idea how important school lunches are for the students here?" he asked.

I told him I had some idea.

"Well, here you are! Bringing in beans and bread."

He made it sound as bad as the school lunches really were! I got suspended for a week from school for creating a lunch strike. After that, some people nicknamed me "The John L. Lewis of Warsaw" after the famous leader of the United Mine Workers of America.

One really good thing that came out of the strike was that the lunches changed for the better. Once they saw that no one was eating school lunches anymore, the vegetable-flavored water changed to real vegetable soup with more vegetables. The hot dogs were real hot dogs and not watered down, and the meatloaf didn't have a bunch of bread in it. There I was, a little third grader bringing beans and bread to school. I had no idea what it would lead to.

The Warsaw Theater photographed in 1926. It was destroyed by fire in 1967.

Saturday Afternoon Movies

My mother's store where we lived was just across the street from the movie theater. I could see the box office from my bedroom window. On Saturday afternoons, they had matinee Westerns. The cost was only 10 cents and because it was so inexpensive, a lot of people attended. Back then, if you found five glass bottles, you could cash them in for 10 cents at the A&P. I loved to go to the movies every Saturday, because I loved horses and cowboys, and of course, because it was so inexpensive.

During this time, pea-shooters, which were nothing but large straws, were all the rage. Some of us boys would go into the theater on Saturday afternoons with our pea-shooters hidden and our pockets full of peas. This was when Black people and White people were segregated. The Black people sat in the balcony and White people sat on the ground floor. My friends and I would go up to the balcony and shoot people down below with our pea-shooters. Sometimes the Black people were blamed for shooting peas at the people down below. When I got a little older, I felt terrible for that. Back then, consequences were not something that us kids worried about. We weren't intentionally trying to get the people in the balcony in trouble. We were just trying to have some fun. It wasn't long before management caught on and my friends and I were banned from the movie theater for a good while.

Mr. W.Y. Morgan was a frequent customer at the store Bill's mother owned, and he was a respected editor at the Northern Neck News, *where he is pictured.*

My Walking Liberty Coin that Walked Away

Mr. W.Y. Morgan was Editor of the *Northern Neck News*. An older gentleman, he always dressed up in a suit with a flower in his lapel. He would walk down from the news office every morning to my mother's store and talk to the girls that worked there. Mr. Morgan was deaf and wore a hearing aid. He'd repeat, "Huh? Huh?" as they spoke to him. They would talk about him behind his back thinking he couldn't hear them. But he could hear them as they gossiped. I could tell by the look on his face. He wasn't as deaf as he acted.

This Walking Liberty half dollar was issued in 1923.

So one morning I pocketed my shiny 50-cent piece.

Like every great magician, I had a beaut. Minted in 1944, this coin showed long-haired Lady Liberty striding toward sunrise. This treasured coin was at the center of my plan.

Mr. Morgan arrived at my mother's store as usual and then left for the post office. But this time, I followed him. When I stepped inside, I was ready. Mr. Morgan got his mail, and then he turned to leave. When he was almost at the door, I dropped my 50-cent piece onto the wood floor and it echoed on the planks as it bounced and rolled to a stop. Mr. Morgan jumped with a start and turned around. He picked up my Walking Liberty 50-cent piece and put it in his pocket.

Forrest Patton Photo

Bill and a young buddy traded bottles for money at Hinson's Lunch on Main Street in Warsaw to buy cigarettes.

Lighting Up Lucky Strikes

Back when I was 8 years old, you could get a penny apiece for glass bottles. My friend J.A. Christopher and I would go into Hinson's Lunch on Main Street in Warsaw, and trade bottles for money to buy cigarettes. After we got our cigarettes, we would go into the woods, down from Northern Neck Electric, and smoke. We would wave our hands back and forth so the smoke wouldn't go up into the trees. We thought if anyone saw, they would think the woods were on fire!

J.A. came up with the idea that we should stash our cigarettes and matches in a glass jar to preserve them. J.A. didn't have to worry so much about smelling like smoke because his parents smoked. But I had to be very careful, since my mother didn't smoke. I would wash my hands really good, chew gum, whatever I could think of, to be on the safe side.

We smoked every chance we got, even behind the baseball grandstand. This went on for years. When I was in high school, we usually had 15 minutes between classes. This presented the perfect opportunity for us to slip out behind the agriculture building and smoke. We knew Principal Hodges often sat at his desk and looked out his window to scan the grounds for any mischief. We knew if he saw any smoke around the building, he'd know exactly what we were doing and catch us in the act. So we were careful.

Well, at some point, we must have gotten careless. We were in the baseball dugout having a nice smoke break. I was just about to enjoy another good toke when J.A. hollered out, "Hodges is comin'!"

Hodges was a tall man, but his frame was bent as he hurried across the field toward us, his arms pumping. I took a quick drag. Then I didn't waste any time extinguishing the cigarette, I just threw it behind me.

"Mr. Bill Northern and Mr. J.A. Christopher! What do you have to say for yourselves?" Behind his black spectacles, his face was boiling red. The dugout resembled the smokehouse at my homeplace in Emmerton.

"Using the team's dugout for your incorrigible activities!" Hodges said. "This time, smoking!" He pushed up his eyeglass frames and then suddenly raised his eyes to look behind me. That's when J.A. yelled, "Fire!"

My cigarette had ignited some leaves. Well, Hodges jumped over and started stomping out the flame. He looked like one of those clogger fellows in the Virginia mountains. He could have been a full-fledged member of the Blue Ridge Thunder Cloggers. Turns out, those black wingtips he always wore had quite a tread.

With the fire put out, Hodges' heat returned. Needless to say, I ended up getting suspended. Again.

Waking Up Warsaw
to Go Duck Hunting

When I was in the seventh grade, my good friend Earl Scott invited me to go duck hunting with him. I was much more interested in hunting quail, but I agreed and we decided to go on the morning of New Year's Eve. That morning, I showed up at the bus station on Main Street at 4:30 a.m. to meet him. The buses came early in the morning, so they were open for business.

As Earl was drinking his coffee he said to me, "Boy, what kind of gun do you have?"

"A 16-gauge shotgun," I answered.

"That should be alright," he nodded. "What kind of shells do you have?"

"I have #8 shot."

Earl shook his head. "That's no good for shooting ducks. You need #4 shot. I can't think of anyone that would have #4 shot for 16-gauge shells."

He thought for a minute, then he exclaimed, "I know! Henry Seward has some. Call him up and see if you can borrow some. I know he isn't going to use them today because he is going deer hunting with Brother Scott and will be using his 12-gauge. Tell Henry you would like to borrow some of his #4 shot shells."

So here it is, 4:30 a.m., and I'm calling Henry to tell him I want to borrow some 16-gauge #4 shot shells. Henry answered, and he sounded sleepy, of course. But he said, "Sure, I will leave them on the front stoop for you." I apologized for calling so early in the morning. He said that was okay.

I went to his house, got the shells quietly as I could, and returned to the bus station to Earl.

Earl looked down at my feet and asked, "What kind of boots do you have there, boy?"

I told him, "Just these. I know they're only just up to

my ankles, but that's all that I have."

"You can't go duck hunting in them, they aren't tall enough," Earl said. "You need waders. Henry has some and he won't need them today, he's going deer hunting. Call him back to borrow his waders."

I called Henry again. I said, "Mr. Seward, I'm sorry to bother you again, but is there any way I could borrow your waders to go duck hunting with Earl today?"

He said slightly agitated, "Sure, Bill, you can use my boots today. I'll leave them on the stoop for you." So I went back to his house, quietly again, and got the boots.

I went back to the bus station and got Earl, and off we went duck hunting. Thank goodness I borrowed Henry's boots because the water would have been over the top of the ones that I had. We never even saw one single duck, but it was fun for me. Just being with Earl was fun.

There was always a New Year's Eve event to mark the annual Warsaw High School Alumni Association Dinner and Dance and that very night, I went. Well, so did Henry and his wife, Odessa, who had been my teacher in the second and seventh grades. She knew me well. After dinner, she spotted me, and crooked her finger to me to call me over. I did as she asked. Then she ordered me outside to a dark side of the building. She bent close and said sternly, "Bill, don't you ever call my house at 4:30 in the morning again or I may kill you!"

Baseball & a Very Bad Bounce

When I was in high school, I was on the baseball team. I was never a starter, but I played second base sometimes. But I looked up to Billy Walker, a guy who was ahead of me by a few grades. Now he was a *really* good baseball player. One day he was taking some batting practice and had some of us kids out there fielding balls for him. He hit a really good pitch down towards second base. I saw it headed my way, high up in the sky over Richmond County. Just as you're supposed to, I got right in front of it. But right about that time the ball took a bad bounce and hit me right under my nose. Slam! It split my lip and broke my nose. My tooth was loose but I didn't lose it. For awhile I didn't want to play any baseball at all. I got over that pretty soon, of course, and went on back.

But that was one of the times I was doing what you're supposed to do: I got right in front of the ball. I just wasn't quick enough to get out of the way of it!

The Heyday & Lowdown
of Warsaw Baseball

Baseball was a very big deal in Warsaw, Virginia, back in the mid-1940's. The stands seated about hundreds of people and it was usually standing-room-only. It was definitely the Heyday of Warsaw. Warsaw and Tappahannock were cross river rivals and in the beginning, they had all local players on both teams. But as the rivalry heated up, one of the counties decided to hire a pitcher from Richmond as a professional ringer. This pitcher was way above the local players and was able to strike players out often. By the time the next game rolled around, both teams had hired pitchers and catchers from Richmond, trying to out-do one another.

Tricks to Help 'em Win

I was a bat boy at the time and I recall Warsaw hiring

Jim Trexler and Dewey Wilkins, both pitchers from Richmond that had played professional baseball. Obviously, they outclassed the local batters. These professionals had tricks to make the ball curve more. One of the pitchers had sewn a bottle cap into the side leg of his uniform in order to "rough up" the baseball. The other player had a piece of sandpaper sewn into his uniform, which gave the ball a better spin.

When I wasn't working as a bat boy, I chased foul balls. They paid us 25 cents per ball for every one we returned. Aubrey Lee Edwards' house was right next to the ballpark and when a foul ball would go over into his yard and I ran after it. For some reason, his bulldog tried to bite me every single time. I also sold drinks at the games and as I can recall, some nights I made 10 dollars or more.

Tappahannock hired a player that was retired from the New York Giants. Thompson, I believe. The rumor was they paid him $5,000 just to come and play one game.

Rivalry costs a lot of money!

When he came up to bat, everyone usually anticipated a home run, and he didn't disappoint! He came to bat three times and hit three home runs out of the park! One of them went over the center field fence. Tappahannock had more wealth at that time and usually ended up with the better players. Eventually, they made an agreement that there would be no more professional players hired on either team. Within a year or so, the fans started to lose interest and attendance dwindled to the point to where the events were no longer profitable. Eventually, big time baseball around Warsaw came to an end.

Coming Down with Measles – *Sort Of*

When I was in high school, there were sometimes food fights in the cafeteria. For some reason, I always seemed to be involved in them. Our cafeteria was a multi-purpose room, so it was used for other things like the gymnasium, meetings, etc. After eating lunch, the students usually had to move the tables and chairs.

One day, we were having a food fight and Principal Hodges came in and caught us. He fussed at us and made all of us clean up all of the food on the floor with brooms, dust pans, and mops. After he left the cafeteria, we got into another kind of fight with wet towels. We started snapping wet towels at each other, and naturally, the water in the towels flung bits of food with each snap. Hence, I had dirty spots on my face. A teacher caught us fighting with the towels and asked us to stop and continue to clean up our mess. When we returned to class, the teacher noticed that there were spots on my face. She was afraid I had measles and sent me to Mr. Hodges for verification. Because of his frustration with my classmates and me, Mr. Hodges gladly sent me home with "measles." When I arrived at home that day, my mother wondered why I was home so early. I told her I had the measles. She took one look at my face and sent me walking up the street to see Dr. Sisson. He took one look at me and got a damp cloth and rubbed my forehead, and he said, "This isn't the measles. This is dirt!"

I got suspended for three days for that one.

Altering Time – *Almost*

When I was a senior in high school, there was a high school junior named John Tayloe. It was end-of-the-year exam time. John, myself, and around six others were in geometry class together. On this particular day, our geometry exam was scheduled for after lunch. We were waiting for Principal Hodges so we could take our exam but he still hadn't shown up. John went over and peeked in the window and saw that Mr. Hodges was still speaking to the orientation class in the gymnasium. We figured we would never get to finish our final exam, so somehow we decided we should change the master school clock.

With Principal Hodges occupied, we sneaked to the office where the master clock was. John stood on my back and set the master clock ahead so that it read 30 minutes later than it really was. We hurried back to class, and twenty minutes later, Mr. Hodges appeared with our final exam. But soon after, the bell rang and everyone thought school was out. John and I took off, knowing we were in trouble, because while we'd been changing the clock, we were spotted by a fourth grade boy. All the kids were looking for the buses that weren't there, and everything was pure chaos. At that time, all we cared about was getting out of school.

But that evening around 8 p.m., the phone rang and it was Mr. Hodges, calling me to explain the seriousness of what we had done and expressing his disappointment with me. Not only had we embarrassed him in front of the new students, but we had risked the lives of the first graders because, he said, "They could have gotten run over"! We had thrown a monkey wrench into the entire afternoon and he was very upset with us. The last thing he told me was "Forget about graduating!"

Mr. Hodges called on Friday night and said that we could come back and take the exam the next morning, so we did. The next day was graduation and I didn't know whether or not I would be able to graduate. Finally, around 6 p.m., just an hour before graduation. Mr. Hodges called me to say I could graduate. I believe that once he thought about it, he realized he didn't want me to come back to school for another year. I was so happy to graduate!

Drums, Guns & College Girls

I went off to college at the University of Richmond where I played drums in the band. It really irked me that in the wintertime, when the weather was cold, the band had to practice outside in the rain and snow, while the football players, the big tough guys, got to go inside the gym to practice.

One day we were there, playing our instruments in the snow. Of course the band had to deliver the half time show and then just sit there in the stands. We were in the stands freezing and the football players who weren't playing were on the sidelines wearing big parkas. They had heaters going all down the sidelines to keep them warm, and we didn't have anything. That just kind of rubbed me the wrong way, so it

53

didn't bother me to no longer play in the band when I left school.

I was also on the school's rifle team. My father had taught me how to shoot a shotgun before he died, so I felt comfortable shooting. Besides, some of my friends from home were also on the team.

I left that university, but I stayed in Richmond making a living selling various items door-to-door. Then a friend from school, Mick, got a job with the state highway drafting department and he told me they needed more help. I knew nothing about drafting, but got the job. The drafting office was on an upper floor, across the street from a hospital nursing school. So we each took desks by the window and watched the girls sunbathing on the roof of the hospital.

I kept the job until September, then went to Lynchburg College in Lynchburg, Virginia, and stayed there almost a year. Ann wrote me a letter telling me she was pregnant. I didn't finish school, but left and got married. Of course, then I had to go to work.

Landing in the Big City

Restaurants & the Stock Market

Tasty Freeze Restaurant in Tappahannock had always closed for the winter because all they sold was ice cream. Well, one day the fellow who owned the place decided he wanted to start selling hot food and stay open during winter months. Since I had job experience, he hired me to get the new venture up and rolling. Then another fellow down in Kilmarnock was supposed to open up a Dairy Queen. But just before it opened, he had a heart attack. So they asked me to come down and open it, which I did. In the meantime, I still really wanted to be a full time restaurant manager, so I applied for a job as a manager trainee with Hot Shoppes in Washington D.C., a company that later became Marriott. They hired me.

Landing in Washington D.C.

That drove me to Washington, under the impression that they hired me into a management training program. But the first week's paycheck wasn't what I thought it was supposed to be. They told me when I questioned them that they didn't have me in a management training program, but rather, they needed to watch me work for a couple months to make sure I could do things, see how well I did. Only then would they put me in a management training program.

Well, I stayed there two months and they still had excuses as to why I wasn't on a full manager track, yet they asked me to stay a little while longer. I stayed three more months and it was the same. They still had me as a Curb Manager. I think it was because I was doing a good job in a position where they'd had problems for a long time so they wanted to keep me there. But I was unhappy with that and I left.

Philosophy & the Market

That's when I went to work for Eddie Goldberg at the Bonifant Street Bowl, a duckpin alley. The fellow who was manager was H.P. Stone. I got along real well with "Stoney," as I called him. A lot of people didn't like his demeanor because he was grumpy, but it suited me just fine because I was too. He always told you exactly what he thought, and you always knew where you stood with him. I liked that job because I got to do a lot of reading there, and we read a lot of the classics and a lot of books on religion. That kind of got me to the point where I better understood the world. Well, I thought I did anyway.

At this time, bowling was really picking up, so I bought some stock in AMF and Brunswick, manufacturers of bowling products. Within a year or so, I sold both of them for a really nice profit. From this, I thought I knew what I was doing in the stock market. So I took that money, and I bought some shares in Boeing Aircraft. But instead of going up, it slowly went down and down until finally one day, I decided it was time to let it go, and I sold it. The day after I sold it, the Russians announced they had shot down CIA operative Francis Gary Powers in the Lockheed U-2 plane over Russia. Of course, Boeing Aircraft stock just shot up after that, like all defense industry stocks.

But that taught me a good lesson in the stock market. I learned I really didn't know what was going on there and that I'd been lucky to have made that money before.

Bowling & Hot Shoppes

While I was with Eddie Goldberg, some nights, I also worked for Hot Shoppes as a Curb Manager at different stores to relieve people. I thought it was very ironic because now I could demand the salary I wanted and they were paying me twice as much to come in as relief as they were paying me when I was working full time! However, I got tired of jumping around. Eddie Goldberg started Bowl America, a chain of bowling alleys so I went to work for them filling in at different locations where they needed help. Then Eddie opened the one in Silver Spring, which was really big, I think 120 lanes.

Bonifant Street Bowling Lanes had closed so Stoney went to work as manager of the Silver Spring location and I'd visit him there.

Good Friends in a 'Stoney' Business

It was all my fault so I can't blame Stoney. I was looking for a business to go into, and saw this ad in the paper for artificial stone. Actually it was just a colored concrete and you put it in molds and then placed it on the walls of buildings. This had gone over extremely well in Baltimore. I mean, there were hundreds of houses in Baltimore that had this artificial stone. We thought for sure it would go over well in the Washington area. However, as it worked out, while Stoney and I were good friends, we weren't good business people. I was better at selling, and I wasn't any good at construction. On the other hand, he wasn't any good at selling, but he was good at construction. We tried to butt into each other's part and by the time we figured out that one person needed to do one thing and one do the other, we were broke.

So Stoney went back to work for the bowling alley again and I went to work for Howard Johnson's.

The Clumsy Mare
& a Canadian Deadbeat

My old friend Doc MacDonald knew a fellow by the name of Charlie Finn. Charlie Finn had inherited a farm over on the Eastern Shore from the lady that he had taken care of. Also, he had sold the farm which became the Landover Mall in Maryland. Doc talked Charlie into selling me one of the horses. Charlie had three Standardbreds. One was a three-year-old, Rapid Hanover. We called her Rapid Miss. Doc talked Charlie into selling me Rapid Miss, a jog cart, and a harness for $300. I was able to talk one of the local trainers in Warsaw to get the horse and break it for me. The plan was that I would then bring her to Rosecroft and take over from there. Well, while they were training this poor mare, she went over backwards and broke her tail.

Of course, I didn't know anything about communicating with horses yet. Wouldn't know that for a number of years.

But they brought her up to Rosecroft and I tried to hook her to the cart and walk her to the track. She just wouldn't walk to the track. She kept rearing up in the air and she'd fall over backwards. The people there at that time were really nice and they would help me.

If you could lead her to the track, she'd go around it, but sometimes, she just went right over the guard rail on the inside carrying me with her. I was lucky I didn't break something. Each time, of course, she followed the cart and ran away. But I got up every morning, went out there and tried to help. I left home at 5 o'clock in the morning, went out to Rosecroft--snow, sleet, whatever. I went out there every day and jogged her.

The Rosecroft Side Wheelers

Finally springtime came, and we had a group there called The Rosecroft Side Wheelers. This was a group of race

64

fans started by me and a fellow by the name of Leonard Payne
who was the Public Relations man at Rosecroft at the time.
We thought it would be a good idea to have a group like this to
get people interested. We had drivers and trainers come and
speak, and we went down to the track kitchen and had
breakfast – stuff like that. We also had dinners in the club
house. One of the members of the club was Oswald. One day
he watched me jog a horse named Cisco. He told me that his
brother trained Standardbreds up in Canada and he wanted to
buy her for his brother. That suited me fine, I was glad to get
rid of her really, so we made a deal where he was supposed to
pay me $600 for this horse. One day he came by Howard
Johnson's where I was working and said, "The truck is there
to pick the horse up but we need the papers."

I said, "I'll give you papers, sure. But I need a check."

He said, "I'll tell you what: I don't have my checkbook
with me, but if you'll give me the papers now, I promise you,
I'll bring you a check tomorrow."

I believed him. He took the horse on up to Canada.

But days passed. Still no check. He kept saying his brother hadn't paid him.

So my wife and I decided to go up to Canada to see if we could collect the $600 he owed us. We went to the track up there, just across the border. We caught up with him in the morning and he invited us to come in his trailer for a cup of tea. I've never seen as many flies as were in that trailer. Flies were everywhere. And they were just all over you from the time you walked in the door.

And the supposedly white cups that he gave us tea in were brown from age. Neither my wife nor I could drink the tea. Still, he kept giving us all kinds of excuses for why he couldn't pay. We left without our money.

So that was my first experience with a horse and it didn't work out too well. Doc MacDonald had been helping me with this and he was sorry I didn't get paid. But actually, it was me who felt sorry for Doc because his wife was a real strict Baptist, so she wouldn't let him get too involved racing horses. In addition, he had bought his son a farm in Frederick,

Maryland, with the idea that he would be able to go out there and train a couple of horses with his son. But his son's wife didn't like anything to do with racing, and it got so she wouldn't even let Doc come out there because she didn't want him to influence her husband to get interested in racing.

But Doc could work with me when I worked with horses, so he did, and we're good friends.

My Own Business:
Wardico's First Days

After my job at Howard Johnson's, I was the first person to have a coffee service in the Washington D.C. area and also I sold vegetables wholesale for Mandis and Company, who serviced restaurants, hotels, etc. Ed Cohen was the food service manager of Kahn's Department Stores in the area. He ordered vegetables from me for the lunch room in four of the stores. Ed told other stores where to purchase their vegetables, and that was me. One day, while I was talking to him, I told him about my coffee service business. He asked a lot of questions and decided he would put my coffee brewers in each store in the break rooms. Mandis delivered my coffee along with the vegetables to Ed's stores for me. It was a win-win situation for me.

But I wanted to move back to Virginia, and I told Ed.

He asked me what I was going to do. I told him I didn't know.

He asked me to bring him a phone book from the area, as he

was going to look through it to see if there was a suitable

business that I could start. I took him the phone book the very

next week. After studying the book and considering my

background, he told me his cousin had invented Endust and

had a janitor supply business in Maryland, Daycon. There

were eight janitorial supply companies listed in the phone

book for that geographical area. The closest one was 50 miles

away in Richmond. Ed told me, "If you are willing to work

hard, and I know that you do, you should be able to make a

living right in your area."

That was the start of Wardico, Incorporated, a

janitorial supply company in Warsaw, Virginia. Ed said he

would ask his cousin to come down and get me started. Bobby

Cohen, the son of the owner of the company, came down and

brought me a truck load of what he thought I should sell. The

agreement was that he would take back whatever we didn't

sell. This went on monthly for a few months and Bobby saw what we were selling and made arrangements with the manufacturers to sell to me direct. I started buying from most companies direct and Bobby didn't send a truck anymore. I never did have a personal relationship with Bobby Cohen; it was just a good business relationship.

Credit Where It's Due

In the course of my business, I had two uncles and one of them was giving Wardico a lot of business. They had a large restaurant and he was spending somewhere in the neighborhood of, roughly around $100,000 dollars a year with us.

My other uncle didn't have quite as big a business but they both were very supportive of me and my business and they tried to help.

Both my uncles talked to other business people to encourage them to buy things locally rather than buying things from Richmond and Norfolk like they had been doing for years. Their help was very worthwhile.

Wooden Nickels and Wardico

I was looking for some sort of advertising promotion and one day I came up with the idea that we could give customers wooden nickels to exchange for a discount on the check at local restaurants. We organized it with a few of the restaurants that we would pay them 50 cents for each wooden nickel that our customers brought in. Basically, when we called on a customer, we gave them a wooden nickel, to say, "Thank you for your business and have a cup of coffee on us." So if a customer got five dollars worth of food, then the customer left the restaurant ten wooden nickels. This promotion ended up lasting a year and it was successful. A lot of people didn't cash in their wooden nickels for whatever reason, but it was successful from our point of view for getting our name out there. Plus, it created a lot of good will. That was all that mattered.

Good Friends
Are Good for Business

Growing Alliances

I had a coffee service business in Washington D.C. for a time, and Jimmy James was one of my customers. I became friends with Jimmy and started going with him to the Chi-Am Lion's Club in downtown Washington. One day when my business needed some Styrofoam cups, I noticed that S. Freedman & Sons Paper Company was just down the street from the Lion's Club, so I ordered from there. When I picked up my order, I met Mark Freedman, the son of the founder, and we hit it off.

Not long after that, I opened up my janitorial supply

business, Wardico Incorporated, and forged a helpful business

arrangement with Mark. He already had a Freedman & Sons

Paper truck going to Richmond. I convinced him that since I

was only 50 miles south of Interstate 95, he could put some

items for me on his truck to help fill it up. Mark was especially

helpful to me as far as business was concerned because he had

a first-hand connection with some major companies. In

exchange, since I was already in the janitor supply business, I

was able to help Mark choose the good companies in that

corner to do business with. Our business relationship lasted

for a long time.

But we were good friends too. Mark would come down

with his family and spend a day at the farm fishing on the

pond and walking through the woods. They all seemed to

really enjoy it, including his wife, Eileen because she could

bring her dog with her. He was a German Shepard named

Geddi and he loved to swim. But I had a pet beaver named Sam and Geddi was afraid of Sam, who loved to swim too. That big German Shepherd would have a blast in the water swimming until little Sam came around. Then he would swim the other way!

The Day I Found a Body in Tappahannock

I had a pretty good birddog and one day I went bird hunting with Roger Andrews and his friends Floyd and Otis. Floyd was a dedicated hunter, like no one I've known before or since. And a few days earlier, old Farmer Ware had given Roger permission to hunt his land in Tappahannock, just across the river from Warsaw. So we decided to hunt there.

The property had a typical two-story farmhouse with a shelterbelt of trees around it to keep the wind out. Almost as soon as we turned the dogs out of the car, they stood birds. However, the dogs were pointing exactly at the house. We talked it over and decided to go around to one side of the trees so we wouldn't be shooting at the house. We flushed the birds so that they flew across the field, away from the house. We took some good shots. Floyd and Otis thought that they had killed a bird so we went looking.

Instead, we found the body of Farmer Ware, the man whose farm we were hunting on. He was stretched out in the grass, absolutely still. We were afraid we had killed him because of where his body was located.

But there was no blood. It was clear he had not been shot. I said, "Maybe we should call the Rescue Squad!"

Floyd stooped down to feel the farmer's neck to check for a pulse. Then he said, "It's no use calling the Rescue Squad now. He's cold. Been dead for some time."

I looked down at Floyd and Farmer Ware, then at Roger and Otis. "We better find a phone!" I exclaimed.

Floyd stood up and rubbed his chin thoughtfully. He said, "Let's go on and finish huntin' the place. *Then* we'll call 'em!"

The Last Time I Went Duck Hunting

Pete and Buddy Delano had a fishing boat. When fishing season was in, they would often take me fishing with them. By now I had learned most of what I needed to in order to duck hunt. I had my #4 shot. I had found a second hand pair of hip boots. The fellow sold them to me for only a couple dollars so I didn't have a whole lot of money tied up in them. Now all I needed now was someone to take me duck hunting with them. One day close to Christmas, Pete asked if I wanted to go duck hunting soon.

"Morning or afternoon?" I asked. Neither one of us was a morning person.

Afternoon, he said.

So on Christmas Eve, he picked me up at 2:30 in the afternoon. He was excited. "The tide will be just right," he assured me. "It'll be coming in and we'll get our share of ducks."

We loaded all the decoys and gear into the boat, then we drove it to a little pond outside of Warsaw on Catpoint Creek. We got our seats out in the blind. We were ready. I didn't see a duck in sight. But Pete was confident. "This is perfect!" he said. "In an hour, the tide will be coming in and there will be plenty of ducks."

However, an hour later, the pond seemed to be getting smaller. "I don't know what's happening," Pete said. "The tide should have come in by now."

I was shivering. Then it started to get dark. At this point, I was ready to quit. "Pete," I said, "there isn't enough water in the pond to drown in!"

Finally Pete was ready to admit that the tide wasn't coming in – it was definitely going o*ut.* He said, "I must have looked at the tide chart wrong."

The sun was fading fast behind the horizon across the Rappahannock. We began to pull the decoys in. But the only light we had was Pete's flashlight. It helped a little that they were all tied together. But there wasn't enough water to float the boat. We tried to push it, but our feet got stuck in the mud. We tried lifting the boat up a little, but as we did that, our feet sunk deeper and further into the mud. It took us four hours to get the boat back to where we had parked the car. By then, we were both worn out. We finally made it home before midnight. Our wives were worried sick.

Needless to say, that was the last time I went duck hunting.

Annamae Sanders
& Her Angry Oyster Stew

This was back when Pete Sanders was teaching school.
Most days after school let out, he would come and catch up
with Earl and me and we would all go hunting. His wife,
Annamae didn't eat until a little bit later so it usually worked
out.

Usually.

See, Pete never was in any hurry to quit and go home
for dinner if we were bird hunting or drinking beer. Earl and I
would be ready to leave and get home by 5 o'clock but Pete
would always want to hunt one more field, or have another
beer, or do something together.

So one night we came back after being out hunting all
afternoon. My wife usually wanted to eat by 5:30. But this

night, Pete wanted to stop off somewhere to drink a beer. Then he wanted to talk, and then he wanted to drink another beer. So we didn't get back to Pete's house until around 6:30.

This time, Earl and I had a joke planned. Maybe teach Pete a lesson. So we walked on into the house with him. I found Annamae was in the kitchen. I told her, "Pete's kept us out all night and we want oyster stew!"

Annamae looked at the three of us real funny.

I kept on. "I mean it! I'm ready for some good homemade oyster stew," I said. Annamae laughed a little bit.

But then I sat down at the table.

Annamae marched over to the refrigerator and pulled out a quart of oysters and threw them in a pan. "Alright, you want oyster stew, that's what you're going to get," she said.

Our joke had backfired. In unison, Earl and I said, "No, no! We were just joking."

"Don't you dare leave!" Annamae commanded. "You wanted oyster stew, and that's what you're going to get. Just sit right down at this table and you're going to get your oyster stew!"

Well, I didn't make it home until about 8:30. My wife

had been looking for me and was some kind of mad. But right

to this day if I mention anything to Annamae Sanders about

oyster stew, everybody knows what we're talking about.

Getting Lucky at
the Car Races

When I was in high school, I had a girlfriend named Betty Oakley who had a sister named Vanelia. I used to go to the car races in Richmond with their brother, Newton. I enjoyed it, and it was a lot of fun, but I never got the car racing bug like other people did.

However, one morning 30 years later, I was reading the Sunday paper and saw that the races were in Richmond that very day. Instead of going to church, I spontaneously decided I was going to go to the car races. When I approached Mechanicsville, I saw a long line of cars to my right. I had no idea what was going on, but when I got to the stoplight, I turned right, towards the racetrack. As I drove down Laburnum Avenue, there was another long line of cars on the right hand side of the road, and I had no idea why. I never thought that they were all going to the racetrack. I kept going down that road. There is a road near the fairgrounds that, if you turn right, will take you to the fairgrounds. I knew that the races were at the fairgrounds. I turned into the fairgrounds, and the person behind me let me get in front of them. I looked back and a policeman stopped the vehicle behind me, I was the last car that they let into the on track parking lot. The others had to go to another special parking lot and get on a bus to be driven to the races. I got lucky! So after I parked the car, I found the ticket booth. I approached the cashier and told him that I would like to buy one ticket. He looked at me kind of funny and said, "Sir, this race has been sold out for months!" I wasn't quite sure what I was going to do, I had driven an hour to come to see the races. Right then, a man approached me and said, "I have an extra ticket. My friend wasn't able to come and if you want to buy it, I will sell it to you for exactly what I paid for it," which was $40. I hesitated but he said it was a good seat high up in the grandstands, so I could see the race pretty good. He seemed like a nice fellow, so I accepted his offer. I got into my seat and realized I was hungry. I asked the people next to me where the nearest snack bar was. They shared all of their food with me, fried chicken legs, potato salad, dinner rolls, and more. I didn't need to go to the snack bar. I got lucky again! The experience was a little different than I had remembered. The track had gone from a half mile track to 5/8 mile and the noise from the cars bothered me more than before. The smell of burning rubber didn't appeal to me either. I really enjoyed the people more than anything, especially their kindness and generosity. For someone who hadn't planned to go to the races, and had no idea how it all worked, I was blessed right from the start.

A year or so later, my wife Ann and I were eating at Bill's Barbecue in Mechanicsville and there was a contest to win free tickets to the car races. We went ahead and registered. Who would have guessed? A week before the race, Bill's Barbecue called to say we had won.

So Ann and I planned our trip to the car races. We decided we'd pack a cooler, and I mapped out a great short cut. On race day, with our cooler already loaded in the car, we stopped at Bill's Barbecue, and picked up our tickets. I had my short cut all ready – I took Pole Green Road.

Some short cut that turned out to be! We ended up spending three hours in a long line of cars. The officers were focusing more on moving the traffic on Laburnum Avenue. We missed an hour of the race just sitting in traffic. Then I had to park in a distant parking lot and we missed another half hour of the race.

As we made our way through the gate, I told Ann, "Well, at least we have good seats!" But when we got to our seats, people were already sitting in them. I had to ask them to scoot over. They weren't too happy about that and there was a ruckus. Unfortunately, this day at the races was nothing like the previous one.

The moral of this story? Sometimes it is best to just go and *not* plan.

The Flying Saucer
of the Northern Neck

Ann and I were returning from a concert in Richmond. It was a perfectly clear night and the stars were shining bright. There were other lights here and there from airplanes, passing cars, and the like. I started to tease her. "Look! There's a flying saucer!" Just joking around. "See that? Aliens!" We were having fun on the hour-plus drive.

But when we were almost home, she saw a bright light in the sky. Ann watched it as I drove. Suddenly she exclaimed, "It isn't getting smaller! It's getting bigger!"

I couldn't see it at first. Then all of a sudden, a huge light appeared to be coming right at us, sort of like a huge camera flash. I pulled over under a tree and we just sat there as this light came right for us. The sky got bright for an instant. Then all of a sudden, it disappeared. We sat there trying to get ourselves together before we started back home.

After that night, I had no doubt: flying saucers exist. They might be closer than you think!

Enjoy the following chapters from Bill's debut book as thanks and as an invitation to read *That Yank With the Crystal.*

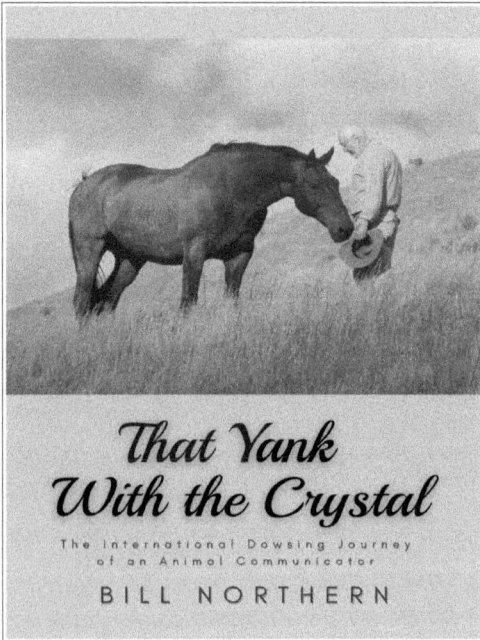

My First Days of Dowsing

One day at my store, Wardico, both bathrooms stopped up. When you have three women working for you, you must have bathrooms! I called all three local plumbers and they could not get to it for at least one week. I knew that there was a cut-off outside of the building, but I wasn't sure where the sewer line was.

So I called the Town of Warsaw and asked them if they could come out and help me locate the sewer line. Since they were just across the street, they came right over with an electronic unit and found something, but it wasn't what we were looking for. So they came back with another tool and they found something, but it still was not what we were looking for.

Next they came over with "L-rods." These are metal rods that are shaped like an L. It turns out that where the L-rods crossed was exactly where the sewer line was. I asked them if I could try and they handed me the L-rods. Sure enough, they worked for me, too! I was so excited. Since the second grade, I had wanted to do something like this. I had tried by using tree branches and it never seemed to work for me. I probably wasn't holding them correctly. The town had a plumbing snake and since the blockage was outside the building, they cleared it for us.

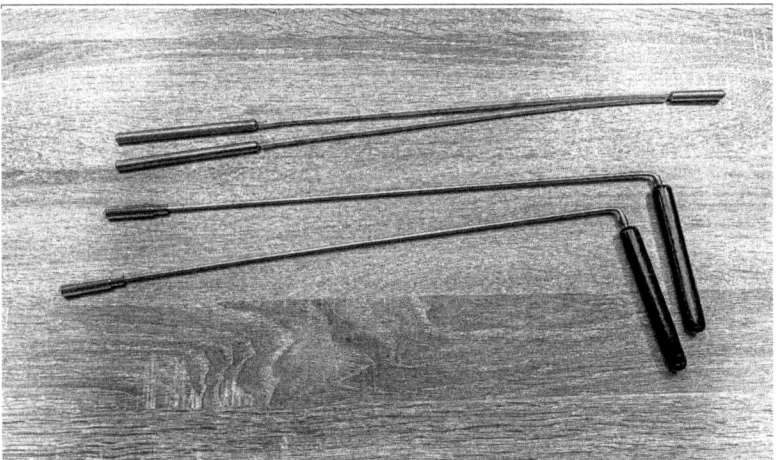

Pictured are two divining Y-rods (top) and two L-rods (bottom) used by dowsers. Photo by Alexandre Linon/Shutterstock

A Journey Begins at the Warsaw Library

That same day, as soon as the town people left, I went to the local library and picked up a couple of books on dowsing. One of the books was *The Divining Hand* by Christopher Bird. The other book noted that there that there was an American Association of Dowsers and they had a convention in Vermont every year. I wrote to the association the next day and asked for more information. I found out that the convention was held every year and now was being held in Lyndonville, Vermont. I found out the details and sent in my deposit right away. It was held in the month of August and I was really looking forward to this trip.

1994 Dowsing Conference in Vermont

We had to fly into Burlington and then drive two and a half hours away to get to Lyndon State College, where the convention was being held. We first went to the hotel and checked in, then we went to the college and picked up our credentials for the next day. When the dowsing classes started.

The first two days were a Basic Dowsing Course and on the first day, we spent all morning listening to people talk about dowsing. It was actually kind of boring to me. In the afternoon, they handed out divining L-rods to all of us and we could go out and find different things on the campus, like water lines, electric lines, etc.

The next day was more serious. We were given a map of the campus and we were expected to mark on a map where the electric and water lines were. Then we brought the maps back to the instructor for a grade. Then, we were given the job of finding any shorts in the wiring of the buildings. We had to walk around three buildings and see if there were any places where the wiring was not installed correctly. Ann and I were able to locate where the wiring was not done correctly right off the bat. Then they gave us the fuel lines that ran underground to find and we were supposed to mark them on a map, too. I don't recall finding all of them, but we found some of them. We received a diploma that said that we had passed Basic Dowsing School. The certificate was signed by the three teachers.

A Life Changing Moment for Bill

The next day was a true life changing moment for me: A lady brought in two horses. This was the first time that they had ever allowed anyone to bring in horses and they have not done it since. There was a group of students and we were standing approximately 200 feet away from each horse. We had a list of 20 questions, the same question for each horse. The questions were included:

Does this horse like women?

Does this horse like children?

Does this horse have a bowed tendon?

Does this horse have a sickle hock?

Does this horse like to swim?

Like jumping?

Like to pole bend, barrel race, dressage?

We had two sheets, one sheet for each horse. We were all using either our pendulums or our L-rods to answer each question. Since the horses were so far away, you couldn't see them to tell whether or not, for instance, they had a bowed tendon. So you had to rely solely on your pendulum or L-rods. I didn't do so well; I think I got five right on one horse and seven right on the other one. This was my very first day of dowsing and as usual, I was a very slow thinker.

That night, I began to think about all of the people that got 17 or 18 right. Most of them were from New York City and probably didn't know a horse from a cow so they *had* to be relying on their dowsing tool. Once this happened, I realized that although I owned horses, I didn't truly *know* them. I was paying around $2,000 per month in veterinarian bills and they didn't really know any more about where my horses hurt than the trainer did. This was when it hit me and I realized that this is what I had been looking for all of my life. I could take the guesswork out of diagnosing the problems with horses and all animals and save them from having to put up with an unpleasant trip from the vet and also, in many cases the owners could save thousands of dollars.

Straight From the Horse's Mouth

The year was 1994-95, and I was at the barn with
Bernice Scott, helping her take care of her brother Herbert's
horses in Warsaw. I walked past this one horse in particular
and heard a voice say, *I didn't get my apple today.*

I looked around to see who had come into the barn. No
one was there. I thought I must have been just hearing things.
Then, a few seconds later, I heard it again, I *didn't get my
apple.* Puzzled, I just stood there and I heard it again, *She
forgot to give me an apple.*

I called to Bernice and told her that Freeholder said he
had not had his apple that morning. She looked at me like I
was crazy and said, "Yes, he did."

Freeholder said in a very sad voice, *No, I didn't either.*

We went on about our day and a little bit later on, it

must have hit her. "Bill, you are right, I didn't give Freeholder his apple! How did you know?"

This was the first time but definitely not the last time, that a horse spoke to me. I had been given a gift!

Dowsing In New Zealand

For many years dowsing or divining was defined as looking for water and pretty much limited to this. Then it was discovered that dowsing could also be used to find deposits of gold and silver as well as gemstones. My first experience with this was listening to some of the old timers in New Zealand talking about how the divines could go to any map of the area and mark the deposits on the map. They would then go to the site to walk over the selected area to find the best place to mine. Later, they could fly over the mountains with their dowsing rods at the area and mark the area that way. In the more modern area, dowsers are used to help locate oil several miles under the surface. There are seemingly no limits to the information that you can gather by dowsing!

Learning to Dowse Horses

The same year I read in the book, *The Divining Hand* by Christopher Bird, I went to New Zealand and stayed a few weeks near Christchurch. I met Fred Fletcher through Sir Roy McKenzie, a noted Kiwi standardbred breeder. Fred trains standardbred horses and also does chiropractic work on them in the afternoon. Fred knew that I had only a little knowledge of horses, even though I had owned, raced and bred them.

One summer evening after tea (every meal in New Zealand is referred to as "tea"), I was teaching Fred how to dowse for water. We were able to find the stream that his well was on, as well as the underground electric and water lines. Fred was a bit skeptical but also impressed that he could locate these with his dowsing rods. We were telling him about all of the things that he could use dowsing for. When I mentioned diagnosing horses ailments his eyes lit up! Fred looked at me and said, "You can do that now."

"Do you really think so?"

"Sure," he said.

'The Yank with the Crystal'

The next morning when I went down to the barn, Fred sent someone out to the pasture to bring in two horses for me to go over. While Fred and the trainer went out training two other horses, I went over the other pair. We wrote down what we found and when Fred came in he confirmed our findings. We were very fortunate to be staying with Faye and Fred as every afternoon people would bring in a few horses for Fred to treat. This was great experience for me as I would stand outside the stall with the pendulum swinging and asking questions of the horse while Fred was going over them with his hands.

Most of the time, after Fred's examination and treatment, he would ask me what I found. We would then have a short discussion before the next horse arrived. Every evening after tea, we would discuss some of the horses that we had worked with during the afternoon. We agreed on most things, but there were almost always some differences. I learned a lot

from these discussions with Fred. In what I do, the way that
you ask the question is very important and Fred helped me
state the questions in a better way. After about a week, people
would ring Faye and ask if the "Yank With The Crystal" was
going to be there. We were fairly busy that year in New
Zealand, but when we returned home in the U.S., no one
would believe that we could actually communicate with a horse
or any other animal. Some actually looked upon it as
"witchcraft." One of my old friends said that when they tied
me to the stake that he was going to "light the first match!"

A Buzz Begins in New Zealand

The next year, our visit to New Zealand was much
more exciting, as a newspaper published a story about us and
we were busy from then until the day we left for home. The
trotting and pacing horses in New Zealand have about four
weeks of stake races beginning in October and ending with
the finals in November. The finals are all raced in what is
called "cup week." The races are held in Christchurch and
horses come from all over the country to compete in these

races.

How a Horse Trainer Became a Believer

One day a trainer that had shipped five horses to the South Island asked me to help him select the best trainer to send each horse to. These horses were all scheduled to race at Christchurch in stake races during cup week.

We dowsed several trainer's names over each horse and came up with the horse's preference. When we were done, I asked the trainer why he chose me to do this for him and why he thought it would work.

He told me a story: He'd used some people on the North Island that did almost the same thing that I did. Using a saliva sample, they would go over, or dowse the horse to find out what was wrong with it. The same as we do. The only difference is they used the radionics machine and I use a pendulum. He was still skeptical back then, so he sent them saliva samples from horses and also himself. In other words, he gave a horse's name to associate with *his own* saliva sample, and sent it in with the rest of the horses' samples.

When the results came back, he went right to the
results of the name that he had used for his own saliva sample.
The report read, "This horse is terribly overweight." (He
weighed about 280 pounds.)

"This horse does not get anywhere near enough
exercise." (He did very little work.)

"This horse seems to be close to someone who smokes a
lot because his lungs are filling with a brown sticky substance.
The person this horse is close to is giving him too much beer
or other alcoholic beverages and it is affecting his whole body,
particularly his brain."

The trainer finished his story to me with a smile and
said, "After that, I will believe almost anything you people tell
me." After reading the report, he had gone on a diet, quit
smoking and drinking, and eventually lost 100 pounds.

A Growing Reputation

We continued on in New Zealand and were going to
horse farms that asked for help with as many as 30 horses. We

were only charging $20 a horse at a time. These breeders would usually ask us to select the yearling fillies that we thought would make the best broodmares. We were actually very good at this. Our demand was growing on the South Island but we were not known on the North Island yet.

Business was still very slow in the U.S. There was a standardbred trainer in Warsaw, Virginia, that would let me go over his horses anytime I wanted, but he did not want to pay for my services. I kept thinking that he would see the value of what we were doing, but if he did see the value he never let us know it. The third year, I told him we would have to charge him $10 per horse and then he only wanted for us to work with one or two a week, but he still expected us to come every day.

This is the end of the excerpt of *That Yank With the Crystal.*

Bill's Angels
Erased My Skepticism

My husband and I have three racehorses in training. Our trainer does her best to make sure the horses are fat, shiny, fit and, most of all, happy. We were winning some races, yet there seemed to be something missing. And what was missing was Bill Northern.

Bill started having "conversations" with these horses about one year ago. At first, we did not think what he was telling us the horses were saying was really so. After all, I was talking with him on the phone, and he was talking to my horse through his Angels. Why would I do something for my horses based on that?

Well, he told me things that only I, my trainer, or the horse would know. Such as: My mare did not like her jockey because during the race, he hit her on the right side, making her sore on that side.

So Bill and I and my mare had another conversation. She told Bill which jockey she liked, and how she wanted to run. She likes to trail the field and come on at the end--and no hitting! We told the new jockey to carry his whip in his left hand, and when it was time for her to make her move, shake it at her. She won by four lengths, and on the backside was six lengths behind the last horse.

That sent me back on the phone with Bill to find out about the other two horses. One of them wanted to run up front. That's not the best place for a distance horse. That horse once had a bad bump into the rail and almost went down, so he wanted to be away from all the other horses. We got the jockey he wanted, and he won.

The other horse, during a conversation with Bill, told him she was sore. So we turned her out for a year. When we brought her back, I got on the phone with Bill. We found her the jockey of her choice, and learned how she wanted to run.

She runs the short distance, and she wants to break easy and settle for a few strides before starting to run. A lot of the shorter races are lost by settling at the break. But we honored how she wants to run. Out of three starts since her year off, she has been second twice, and won her last race by six lengths.

Since I started to listen to what Bill was telling me that my horses were saying, the results have been amazing. We have had six starts. We have been first three times, second twice, and third once, and they all did it their way.

I thank you, Bill. But most of all, my horses thank you.

Ellen Robertson
Leesburg, Virginia
May 2005

My Angels, Dowsing & Communication

Bette the Racehorse Picks Her Jockey & Wins

My clients Helen and Ed Coop had high hopes for their racehorse Bette but she had not been performing well. So we walked down to the paddock and I asked Bette what was going on. She communicated to me, *My jockey is lousy! I'm not going to work hard for him because he doesn't know what he's doing.*

I shared this with Helen and Ed, who admitted the jockey was their trainer's apprentice. After I communicated with Bette, Helen and Ed decided they would not place much of a bet on her today. That was just as well, since she finished near the back of the field.

We went to the clubhouse for lunch. It was a perfect place to watch the races and eat lunch. But Helen kept asking me one question after the next. Finally in desperation I said, "Helen, if you will just let me finish my lunch, I will answer all your questions."

She did give me time and then we had a good talk as I returned to the paddock to be with Bette. One of my good friends and clients, Lynnley Driver, was also racing two horses that afternoon. She was quite busy with her horses as she was the trainer and had to stay close to care for them. It was a sad day for a lot of us, as one of her horses was coming off of the last turn for home, about four lengths in front, when he stepped in a hole and broke his leg. After a long discussion with the veterinarians, it was decided he would have to be put down. We spent a good deal of the afternoon talking about the incident and taking turns crying.

A Turn of Events Helps Bette

The next Monday I was at a thoroughbred farm talking with some yearlings when the subject of Bette came up. The owner of the farm also owned a percentage of Bette and had heard what she told us before the races on Saturday. I told him that I thought by the way she acted that she was not going to try for this jockey. He explained that the jockey was under contract to the trainer to ride his horses and it was a precious little they were going to be able to do about that. When we went in for tea, the gentleman asked if we could connect with Bette and find out which jockey she liked. He named a few jockeys. Most of the jockeys she liked were not going to be available. But she communicated four that she thought were good and would try hard for. He said he would organize one of these to ride her in her next race. However, the trainer and his apprentice would not agree to let someone else ride Bette! Unfortunately for them, the apprentice jockey was in an automobile accident three days before Bette's next race and was injured too badly to ride for a couple of weeks. My client got one of the jockeys that Bette liked. When race day came, she knew she had a good jockey. She was very frisky in the paddock. Bette communicated to me she *could* win because the jockey knew how to ride her. When they came around the last turn headed for home, she was right on the pace and bolted in to win by six lengths.

A Six-Year-Old Trotting Mare

During his recent visit to New Zealand, I sought the assistance of Dowser William Northern to dowse a six-year-old trotting mare in my stable in an effort to improve her trotting gate and race performance. William was very obliging and keen to assist. At the initial dowsing session, he was able to pinpoint areas of pain in the mare's body, most of which had not been previously detected by a veterinary surgeon who had conducted a thorough examination several days prior to William. In fact, the veterinary surgeon was unable to offer any explanation for the mare not performing up to my expectations and her previous indications of above-average ability.

Once William had completed his dowsing, I began to treat the mare based on his recommendations. Within three to four days, her gait and attitude had improved significantly which prompted me to seek William's dowsing ability in regard to the shoes that the mare was wearing. I felt this could also be improved, but I was unsure of what changes if any to make.

William dowsed the mare's shoes, and determined that her hind shoes were suitable, but major changes were needed to her front shoes. Although the recommendations that William's dowsing made were quite revolutionary to say the least, I had already seen beneficial results from the initial dowsing for pain. Therefore, I had no hesitation in adhering to his instructions. Ultimately, the front shoes were changed to the extent that the horse now wears two totally different shoes on the front. On the near-side front, there is a standard five-eighth half-round shoe weighing approximately five ounces. On the off-side front, there is an aluminum shoe with a slightly raised heel and square toe at a total weight of two ounces.

Having regard for the common theory of trotters

requiring perfect and equal weight and balance on both front feet in order to provide reliable performance on the race track, the shoes that this horse now has dismisses this theory as fallacy rather than fact.

I have no hesitation in stating that this mare is now trotting better than ever before, and as a regular driver of her, I cannot fault her gait and balance. It is, in my opinion, as close to perfect as one could get and indeed a direct result of the dowsing recommendations that William provided to me.

Graeme T. Bennett
Christchurch, New Zealand
April 1996

121

Bill Meets Grateful Remote Clients

One of my clients rang and said he had two horses he wanted help with. There was a new American veterinarian in the area so he invited us both to dinner. We went over the horses and then had dinner. The vet was able to locate most of the problems that I found. That is a bit unusual. Dinner was great, but I drank too much red wine so I was pleased to get an offer for a ride home. Just then, a man named Ken Austin rang and said he and his wife would like to drop in once I got there. The name was vaguely familiar but I could not place him. When they arrived, we went to the lounge. He had a large photo of his dog. He told me that the previous year, I had located his missing dog for him. Ken said, "Bill, we lived in Cheviot and you were in Kentucky. You agreed to do this favor for us. Shortly after we emailed you the dog's name and photo along with the address from where he went missing, you marked on a map where you thought he was and sent it to us. You marked on the map, within a foot, of where his body was. He was dead and had been run over by a train. We are very grateful, because without your help, we may never have located him to bury him properly."

Letter From Orana Wildlife Park, Christchurch

We would like to thank you for coming to visit us at the Orana Wildlife Park, and for taking the time to communicate with some of our animals while you were here.

All of the staff found it very interesting, even the skeptics! We are continuing to work with the animals, and are trying some of your suggestions. Ian has taken his mission of continuing his relationship with Stumpy, our lone male rhino, very seriously. He has promised that he will communicate with him about his reintroduction to the females.

Mavara, zebra stallion, seems to be getting an idea about what he is supposed to be doing with/to the females. We *are all hopeful that he will be ready for the "task" sometime*

soon!

We would all love it if you popped in to see us when

you visit Christchurch in the future.

Tara Atkinson
Christchurch, New Zealand
August 2002

The Spiritual Power of Uluṟu

We were visiting Alice Springs, Australia, and decided that we wanted to see Uluṟu/Ayers Rock, a large sandstone formation in the Uluṟu-Kata Tjuṯa National Park in Australia's Northern Territory. In 1985, the Australian government returned ownership of Uluṟu to the local Pitjantjatjara people with the agreement that the park system could lease it. The local people requested that visitors not climb Uluṟu, due to the site's spiritual importance as well as dangers of the climb. But through the years, people continued to make the climb, and some died until climbing was banned a few years after our visit. Home to numerous species of mammals, trees, flowers, and grasses, Uluṟu has always been a sacred place for Aboriginal people who believe their spiritual ancestors live there.

We wanted to see this beautiful landmark. But how? The bus ride was three hours long one way and we didn't want to do that. So we decided that the easiest way to get there would be to take a small airplane. This plane held six people besides the pilot and co-pilot. The flight out to Uluru was good. Climbing was still permitted then, and we walked a little way up. Some tourists walked further than we did.

After our visit, we all got back into the airplane and took off for Alice Springs. About halfway back, with no warning, the plane fell a frightening number of feet in a matter of seconds. It really lost altitude quickly, leaving the pilots scrambling to recover as we plummeted to the earth that not so long ago, we'd been climbing! Even though we had seatbelts on, the drop caused everyone's head to hit the ceiling of the plane. Neither the pilot nor the co-pilot knew what was going on. It seemed as though we were caught in some sort of vacuum. We were all scared. Maybe this hadn't been a good idea!

Then all of a sudden, the plane leveled off and we were flying smooth again. None of us knew what was going on. But we landed safely in Alice Springs. Once we exited the plane, I could see that one couple had wet pants, and one gentleman even had a brown stain on the back of his!

Thinking back on it now, we could have considered the spiritual meaning of Uluru and enjoyed the visit without climbing it.

Pendulum Dowsing for the Missing Wedding Rings

Sometime in the early fall of the crazy year 2020, my friend Larry came to see me in Williston, Florida, about a dilemma. Some time before calling me, he had purchased a wedding ring set from a recently-divorced woman. Now that he had a buyer ready to put down money, he could not find them. He thought perhaps my Angels would be able to help.

Larry explained he'd been carrying these rings around in his truck, hoping to sell them. But in the spring of 2019, he had purchased a new truck and transferred everything from the old truck to the new one. Or so he thought. Now here he was unable to find the set.

"What are the rings in, Larry?" I asked. He described a standard jewelry store box. He thought he could recall putting them on a shelf in his shed. "But I'm not so sure," he admitted.

"I've looked everywhere including my safe."

After Larry left, I got my pendulum. Sitting at my dining room table, I began to look. This is very draining work. I went over his shed, bedroom, kitchen, and living room. I didn't see them anywhere. I kept getting a *no*. The rings were not there. The safe was the last place I looked because it is not large and Larry was positive the rings were not there.

But my Angels disagreed. They said the rings were in Larry's safe. All I had to do was find them. Slowly I looked in every box. Most boxes had ammo and there were guns stored away there. But there was one box which didn't look like it belonged. Inside this box were the ring boxes. The outer box was hidden from view by a larger dark red box.

I called Larry and told him where the rings were. When he arrived back home he had a look and found the rings exactly as I had seen them.

Clearing the Buzzards

Buzzards were covering the water tower in the town of Warsaw, Virginia. *Lots* of buzzards, more than 100 of them. The Mayor at the time wanted them removed because people that drove through Warsaw were starting to call it "Buzzard Town." I went to a Town Council meeting and told them I could persuade the buzzards to move, but it would cost $500. The Council thought that was too expensive. So I forgot the issue until I got a call from my friend, Tom Herbert. Tom told me he had a bunch of buzzards around his pond behind his shopping center right in town, not far from the water tower. He wanted to pay me to clear them. "How about 6 o'clock tomorrow morning?" he asked.

.   "At 6 o'clock in the morning, I'm sleeping," I said.

"How about I meet you there at 6 o'clock tonight?"

"At 6 o'clock at night, *I 'm* sleeping," Tom said.

So I went to the pond right then. Tom had fenced it in, and sure enough, there was a buzzard on each fence post. I counted: 100 posts. So I got to work: I explained to the buzzards they were causing the landowner problems and that there were plenty of pine trees right behind the pond where they could go. When I began to put my hands up to form the energy field around the pond, some of the buzzards left, and some of them started swirling and swooping around me like they were going to attack. So I told them that my energy was much more powerful than theirs and that I was serious about them leaving. Before I left that evening, they were all gone. The next morning, 20 had returned. I told them that they had to leave and they started swooping at me again. I reminded them, again, that my energy field was much stronger than they were and finally, they left. The buzzards never returned to the pond.

They still congregate on the water tower.

My Cockatiel, Poquito

Mr. Northern, You did a reading for my cockatiel, Poquito, who was very sick at the time. I wanted to let you know how well he is doing. All of your suggestions were very helpful, and we are still feeding him a bit of yogurt. The vet is enormously pleased with his progress, and he no longer needs to do weekly antibiotic shots. His last bloodwork came back A-OK for anemia, as well as showing that his white blood cell count was normal – no more infection.

I have been giving him little bits and pieces of the fruits and veggies that you suggested. He eats them sometimes and sometimes does not. I did go out and buy some baby food with the recommended veggies in it, and he wolfs that down out of a little feeding tube. Guess he likes to be hand fed!

He is now one happy birdie. I want to thank you so much for all that you did. I appreciate it so much. And so does my happy birdie, Poquito.

Karia Rossin
July 2002

Emmerson & The Green Monkey

By Billy Herbert

As told to Cesca Janece Waterfield on April 2, 2022

Twenty years ago, we got a puppy for our children. Got him from the SPCA. We named him Emmerson, and he was kind of a Lab and Shepherd mix. He was a great young dog.

But we had a problem when I would go to work and my wife would go to work and take the kids to the babysitter and leave the dog at home: He would chew anything he could get his teeth on. We're talking furniture, siding on the house, electric wires. If he could get his teeth on it, he would chew it. We tried everything. The vet gave us sour apple spray that you could spray on items. Supposedly it tasted bad to the dog, But our dog happened to think it was a candy apple. It didn't stop him a bit.

I knew Billy Northern because we go to church together. I told my wife when we were getting frustrated, "I'm gonna take Emmerson to see Billy. He's kind of weird. I don't understand how he does what he does, but let's give it a try."

My wife wouldn't go. She said, "Take the dog and go."
I called Billy and he said, "Yeah, come on down."
I took Emmerson to the house and Billy did his thing. When I got home, my wife asked, "What'd he say?" I told her one of the things he'd said was Emmerson liked green beans.

She said, "No! That dog doesn't eat green beans. Here, I'll show you." So she got a can of green beans and put them in the bowl. Well, the dog couldn't eat them quick enough. He ate them like crazy!

Billy had also told us, "When you leave in the morning, the dog is afraid that you might not come back. He gets anxious. So take just a couple minutes and tell him you're going to work and you'll be back."

My wife was the Postmaster so she went to work at 4 o'clock in the morning. So we'd tell the dog: "Now Mama's gonna be back at 2 o'clock. You'll be alight till then, so just be calm."

Within 24 hours, that dog made a 180-degree turnaround. We never had another problem with him chewing, we never had another problem with him doing anything, other than he was just a great dog.

Two or three months later, I was going into a restaurant for lunch and I ran into Billy and he stopped me as I was going in and he said, "I talked to Emmerson the other day."

Here I am, I'm still freaked out. I said, "Oh, really? I hope he didn't tell you any family secrets."

Billy said, "No, but he did tell me he really misses his green toy."

I didn't have a clue what that meant. But when I got home that evening, my wife and I were talking about our days, and I told her I'd seen Billy at lunch. I told her, "He said Emmerson misses his green toy." She looked at me, with her jaw dropped a little bit and she said, "Don't you remember?"

And I said, obviously not.

But my wife reminded me that on our way home from the SPCA where we got him, we stopped and got him a plush monkey to play with. He carried that monkey around with him till it was no bigger than a postage stamp. We finally threw it away and I forgot all about that green monkey. But right then and there, I said, "Well, whatever it was, Emmerson misses it."

From that day until Emmerson passed away, he had with him a green plush toy. He didn't really chew on it. He carried it around with him like Linus with his blanket.

The Horse Who Believed a White Lie

My clients Faye and Maria usually ring me before calling the vet because I can usually remotely see where the problem is and that makes it easier for the vet to sort out proper treatment. Three times a year Faye and Maria have me come to their place for an in-person visit. They have seven horses, dogs, cats, birds, and other animals to keep me busy for the day.

A Bit About How I Work

I always try to determine if the horses have any internal problems, lameness, or soreness problems. I ask the horses who they prefer to be turned out with, and then try to arrange the turnout scheme so they are all happy. Like people, horses often change the way they feel about each other and wish to change their friends. They will often be jealous of another horse because he or she gets more attention or is doing better in his work at the time. I also try to see that they are in a stall that suits them. The horses will usually tell me what they like and do not like about the farm, their caretakers, and riders. They are usually most critical about their riders. They tell me what activities they like and which they do not like. They frequently comment on their tack.

Faye and Maria told me how well their horse Chris was doing with their son Adam riding him. They wanted to know how Chris liked his new bridle. Chris communicated to me, *I like the new bridle. But why didn't they buy new lines? The ones I have are very stiff and are hard on me!* I conveyed this to Faye and Maria and they laughed in surprise because they had thought the lines were okay and didn't know Chris wanted some softer ones. I knew they would take care of it!

The Earnest Equine

Earlier that day, Adam, Faye, and Maria had gone to pick up a horse named Teddy from Adam's friend to sell for him. With seven horses of their own, they were short on room at their place. So they had taken Teddy to their neighbor Steadman so that Teddy would be close by for a young lady and potential buyer who was on her way over to ride the horse for a second time. I gave Teddy a quick going-over from a distance and did not find anything wrong. But Teddy communicated to me, *I don't like that girl who's coming to ride me. She's not a very good rider but she thinks she's something great. I really do not want to go to someone like that.*

Soon after, the young lady showed up. Teddy did everything she asked and could hardly have been better. But she wanted to look at another horse for sale elsewhere before deciding. Meanwhile, as Steadman had watched her ride, he had misgivings after hearing the girl say she'd been put on the ground by some other horses. That evening, he called Faye into Teddy's stall, and reluctantly explained that he didn't want to be sued if someone was hurt while riding Teddy on his property. Faye sympathized with her longtime neighbor and didn't want him to feel bad. So she lied, "It's no problem at all!

Teddy has been sold and we'll bring the trailer right over to collect him."

As the three of them took the trailer over to pick up Teddy, I headed home. But the next day, Faye told me everything. In fact, she paid me a compliment: "I've learned a lot from you, Bill!"

Talk to Your Four-legged Friends

When they arrived to collect Teddy, the horse simply would not load onto the trailer. The three of them tried everything to coax him on. Finally, Maria suggested they go home to get some tranquilizer. But Faye thought about it, and back in the truck, she made a connection. "You know, Teddy was standing there when I told Steadman that he'd been sold."

"So?" Maria asked.

"Well, Teddy told Bill he didn't like that girl. He probably wouldn't load because he thinks he's going to her!" Faye suggested they tell Teddy the truth. They got out of the truck and went to Teddy.

"Teddy, you aren't going with the girl who rode you today," Maria explained. "You're really going back to our place with all our other animals and horses."

With that, Maria was able to lead Teddy to the the trailer with no problem. Back at their place, he unloaded just as he should.

This is just one example of why you should always be honest with your four-legged friends.

Ron and Susan Blackburn consulted with Bill before adopting their beautiful cat, Princess.

The Princess of San Antonio

On December 29, 2021, we adopted royalty into the

Blackburn family. But first, we called Bill.

We'd visited the shelter at the Animal Defense League

in San Antonio, Texas, to see if there were any potential cats

we might be interested in adopting. We saw one in particular

who caught our eye, so we took a few pictures of her and sent

them to Bill Northern. We would never make such a huge

decision without his input. Bill got back to us and gave us his

thoughts about her personality and traits. He said she had a

good self concept, and she also felt that she was two steps

above the rest of the cats. With this positive attitude, Bill said,

certainly she wanted a special name. He said she was thinking

about a name connected with royalty, so I emailed Bill a list of

royal titles. She chose Princess, which is very fitting for her.

She sure acts like a Princess! And like the most eminent of nobles, she is getting very spoiled.

Susan Blackburn
Texas
January 2022

Socializing My Stallions

I first heard about Bill Northern when I was looking for someone to help me figure out my stallions' problems with humans. I wrote a message on a horse forum, and a reply came up about Bill with a few web pages to read. Funnily enough, I forgot to follow up as I read that he lived in the U.S. Then at the start of 2004, my boss, the horse physiotherapist, Clare McGowan, asked me if I was interested in this guy talking to my horses. I was keen as they come! In fact, I had several for him to visit. I left a message asking if I could book Bill in to see four horses of mine and two for Clare.

One day, I got a phone call with the only appointment available before Bill left for the South Island, from where he was to fly to Honolulu. The problem was that I was flying out in two hours to Christchurch, and wasn't going to be back until after he had left. Well, after a few phone calls organizing people to pick up my horses and take them to Bill, I hopped on a plane. All afternoon on Sunday, I wanted to know how it was going. My friend Aimee was with Bill and videoed it all for me. She said Bill was amazing. So the next day, I sat and watched it all. I was shocked. He was just standing there next to the horses that had just been pulled out and tied up in front of him. He said things about each horse that you just couldn't guess. Here are the horses, one by one.

Nik, Grey Stationbred Gelding

I was concerned that Nik was getting on in age, and I didn't want to push him if he didn't want to do it anymore. Bill asked him what he liked doing. Nik told him that he wasn't a dressage horse but was a fantastic jumper, and that he was fast and could jump big fences at speed. This is too true. He still wanted to jump! This made my day. Nik refuses to do any sort of dressage, but he'll jump all day. He is the best and safest hunter that you would ever sit on. Nik said that he only likes to do enough dressage to warm up for the jumping.

This is a horse that I can only canter to warm up. He can't
trot properly, so I don't do it. He is happy when I just canter
him around for ten minutes and then start jumping.

Bill asked him why he got nervous at the shows. Well,
Nik said that it's because I get really nervous and that upsets
him. Nik also said that I had to memorize my courses.
Although I don't get lost when I'm going, I do panic about
where the first fence is when I walk in. Bill said that I need a
glass of wine before I compete. Since I can't do that, I take my
Bach Flowers Remedy to chill me out. I only get nervous
because one time, Nik jumped out of the ring and slammed
into a horse and truck at a show. Clare, my horse
physiotherapist, found his neck majorly out ,which caused his
neck muscles to be almost like they had tetanus. Bill said that
he had a vertebrae fused in his neck, and though it didn't hurt
anymore, he still feared it.

Blaze, Bay Stationbred Gelding

This is my Mum's plodder schoolmaster that I steal for
show hunter. Everyone rides Blaze because he is so quiet. I

was worried because I felt that he had recently been going off his jumping. He'd had a major injury in his rear hind which put him out for eight months. Since then, he'd been doing a bit of everything with everyone. This must have confused him because Bill said that Blaze didn't know what his purpose was. Blaze is a funny guy, and he seems so laid back, but actually did get quite wound up and stressed. Bill found an ulcer and recommended yogurt in his diet.

When Blaze was asked what he wanted to do, he said that he wanted a holiday. He liked jumping, but he was sore. He wants to be a dressage horse for a while, because he can really move. This horse has amazing movement. So I have stepped off and given him back to my Mum to do dressage on and cruise. We also have to tell Blaze what he is going to be doing day to day, which has worked amazingly. He doesn't get stressed anymore when we go places. We also told Blaze that his purpose is to look after my Mum, and he'll have a "cruise-y" life.

Kahu, Black and White Pinto Stationbred Stallion

This is the stallion that I wanted Bill to examine all those months ago – a very quiet and spooky guy. Before I got him, he ran wild for 11 years, on the east coast of the North Island in New Zealand. He is the only horse that I can't figure out.

I treat all of my stallions and colts like normal horses and I haven't had problems handling them. The stallions are only separated when breeding season is on. Bill said that Kahu thinks he is just like the others, and didn't know what his purpose was. Straight away I thought, "How the heck do you tell a gorgeous stallion what his purpose is?" We came up with showing him all of his stunning progeny. He didn't know that they were his.

I like to do in-hand showing with him for publicity purposes, but we have always had a problem with finding someone who he likes to lead him. As soon as a leader spooks him or gets angry with him, he refuses to lead. I have always let him choose his leader. Amazingly enough, he is quite particular. It might sound stupid, but it works. I have never really had a good bond with him, so I try to get someone that he likes. He told Bill that he loves me, but doesn't respect me because I have only ever told him when he was bad and never praised him when he was good. Since Bill told me this, I explain everything to him so that he doesn't get confused; he is a changed horse. I haven't quite gotten his whole trust, but it has come a heck of a long way in such a short time. Now I can do anything in the paddock with him without having to put a halter and lead on him. He used to snort all of the time, and he hasn't done that for weeks now. Bill asked who he wanted for his leader, and he chose Clare, my boss, who he absolutely loves. She fixes him up when he strains muscles and hurts himself. So Clare has been booked as his permanent leader at the shows.

Star, Chestnut Former Thoroughbred Racehorse

Bill did this one by remote which I thought, "I'll give it a go; what do I have to lose?" Star was in Pukekohe, South of Auckland in the North Island, and Bill was in Christchurch, 1000 kilometers away in the South Island of New Zealand.

But Bill picked all of his sore spots to a T, including an irritation in his lower left jaw in his mouth caused by a strand of silage that had stuck in his teeth that I had to get out for him. I couldn't believe it. When I got Bill's reading in an email, I was standing next to Star and I was pushing all of these sore spots that Bill had indicated in his email, and they were all there. He made me a total believer then and there.

Bill said that Star was lacking in potassium. This was mind-boggling because when Star was racing, he had to have Standardbred racehorse salts, which are high in potassium compared with the Thoroughbred ones. Star is now getting the dose of Standardbred salts he had while racing. He is laid back again instead of stressed.

When Star was racing, he was quite a maniac on the track. His owner was going to put him down when he retired, until I stepped in. There was no way I was going to let this happen. I get on really well with this horse, and I'm determined to prove to everyone that he isn't nuts. Bill told me that he'd like to do a bit of dressage to keep him in shape and concentrate on hunter jumping. Star has a really good jump, as he proved jumping the odd gate every so often to see his girlfriend down the raceway. So after we get his body and feet right, Star and I will be making an entrance to the show hunter world.

Ivy, Brown Homebred Mare

This horse is owned by the friend I mentioned, Aimee. Aimee had spent all morning telling Ivy not to embarrass her before Bill got there. The first thing that Ivy said was that Aimee was stingy with food. Aimee doesn't feed Ivy every day – I do. She had only given Ivy a snack to keep her occupied in the box for two hours until Bill came. The next thing that Ivy said was that Aimee needed lessons as she had no balance and wobbled all over Ivy's back. That just devastated Aimee. It's hard enough when your instructor tells you this, let alone your horse. This I blame mainly on her saddle which doesn't seem to fit Ivy anymore, as I found when I rode her; it just wouldn't keep still on her back. When I changed the saddle, I was fine. Bill did say that Ivy had a sore back, probably due to the saddle. He also pointed out a sore hock, which we knew of, but hadn't said a word to Bill about.

Bill asked Ivy why we couldn't repeat the same training day after day. Ivy said that it was boring, and that she already knew how to do it. Trust me, I broke this mare in, and she has got to be the fastest learner that I know. She used to throw tantrums if I tried to repeat something that I had done the day before. She is only four years old and first year under saddle, and could just about do most medium-level dressage moves. She thrives on a challenge. The harder it is, the more she loves it. Bill said that we just have to keep it challenging for her. She also kicks the heck out of the stables when we put her in them. Bill told us that she, once again, gets bored, and that we need to give her a mirror to stop her from getting bored. Just what we need – a vain horse!

Bill Northern just said things that were too close to not believe. He is an amazing man, and I would recommend him to anyone. I've spent hundreds of dollars on people trying to find my horses' problems. From now on, if I have a problem that I can't resolve or that Clare McGowan can't fix, I'm ringing Bill.

He is the true "Doctor Doolittle." I'm never going to miss another appointment. Trust me! Thanks, Bill.. We are your friends for life.

Kiri Matenga & Aimee
South Auckland, New Zealand
February 2004

Elephant Friends at The Phoenix Zoo

One year my wife and I were in Arizona for a dowsing conference. While waiting at Hertz to return the rental car, a car packed with children pulled beside us, windows down. They were all talking about the zoo. I asked the driver for directions, got out of the queue to turn in the car, and headed for the Phoenix Zoo.

The Phoenix Zoo is the largest privately-owned, non-profit zoo in the nation. I was excited to visit. So even though it was 3:30 when we got there, giving us only 90 minutes to enjoy, we bought tickets anyway. I told the information booth my name and that I was an animal communicator. I left a business card and went to listen to some animals. We worked our way to the lions, asking each group if they were satisfied with their home. Most were satisfied, some were not.

Not long after, the closing bell rang and we started for the exit. Just then along came a man in a golf cart. He introduced himself as the zoo director. He'd been told I was an animal communicator. He asked if the animals we had seen were happy and I gave him our thoughts. He asked, "Well, have you seen the elephants?"

"We didn't get a chance before closing," I told him.

"Get in!" he said. "I'll take you."

When we arrived at the elephant compound, there were two female elephants there, one African, named Reba, and one Asian, named Indu. Reba and Indu were not very happy. Their area was small, probably a quarter of an acre of usable space for the two of them. Indu communicated that they would like a job to do as they were bored. Each day, they both looked forward to the girl that brought them some hay. The larger elephant tried to keep the smaller one away from the girl. Indu communicated she was sore in the left withers. Reba was sore in the right withers and right front ankle. I sensed that they were low on some vitamins and minerals. I gathered that neither got enough exercise to properly exercise their joints. The director introduced us to the crew and told them I was an animal communicator. Most of them snickered.

But I went to work. The first elephant, Reba, was behind bars next to us, and Indu was out quite a distance from us in the open area.

Reba again communicated that her right front foot was sore. Reba came over to the bars and lifted her foot so that the director and caretaker could see she had something stuck in it. The caretaker came over to have a look but he did not know what the object was. Then Reba turned around so we could see a cut on her hind leg. The caretaker was embarrassed that he'd missed this obvious cut.

Indu was quite a way from us in the outer part of the compound. The caretaker said Indu had recently gotten so that she disliked all humans. She wouldn't allow anyone to come close to her for any reason. Not to feed, bathe, or anything. So I asked her what might be bothering her. She communicated to me, *I'm mad because they took away the red stuff.* I conveyed this to her caretaker.

"Last month we stopped feeding her watermelon because she wasn't eating it!" he said. "But we can return it to her diet if she misses it." I turned to Reba and communicated to her that she would again get the red stuff every day. She was so pleased that she picked up a trunk full of bamboo and headed toward me. The caretaker called out, "Get behind the bars because Reba can get to you!" I did as he said. Reba came over and dropped the bamboo as close to me as she could get.

Next came the bears, Rio and Rizzaro, who seemed very content. Luka, the cub, was up in a tree and really related to my wife more so than me. When we moved away, this one came down and wanted to go with us.

Now the director was naming other animals that needed a little help. We stayed that evening for another two hours. Before we left, he asked us to return the next morning before we flew home. The next day, we arrived early at the airport and checked in for the flight. A driver from the zoo picked us up and took us to work with more animals. We actually stayed so long, we were late getting back to the airport and they were paging us to hurry to our flight.

A Hawaii Attorney Finds His Lost Dog & Discovers His Angels

Bill Northern, who I only discovered after *he helped me find my lost dog, is truly a miracle. My recent personal experience may give hope to other dog lovers who are searching for their lost companions.*

On Thursday, February 26, 2004, lightning and thunderstorms struck Hawaii in the early afternoon. Like every workday, I left my home that morning after securing Buddy, my mixed-breed hound dog around eight years old, in my garage, leaving him a half foot gap in the garage door for ventilation. Buddy is a large, friendly dog weighing about 65 pounds. He is well-mannered, lovable, and a true companion to me and my family. Unfortunately, the thunder must have scared him out of his wits and, in his panic, out of the garage as well. That evening, after an intense search in the neighborhood, he was nowhere to be found.

The area we live in is a gated community located against the Koolau Mountains. The neighborhood is surrounded by a forested ridgeline to the left and a densely forested valley with heavy underbrush to the south. Lately, wild pigs have been seen roaming the streets at night, foraging for food.

When Bud did not return home by the next morning, I knew he was hiding somewhere, but where? I had 150 flyers printed with his photograph and a plea for his safe return. These were distributed throughout the neighborhood, posted at nearby parks and trails, and provided to our local security detail.

My parents own a ranch and board horses in Waimanalo. They love animals, especially horses and dogs. My mother knew Bill Northern was still in town, but was *returning to Virginia soon. Unbeknownst to me, she contacted him by phone and asked if he would assist me in finding my lost dog. He agreed. Bill asked her for my dog's name and my street address. He advised her to tell me that Buddy was alive, scared, and curled up in some bushes about a quarter mile to the right of my garage, assuming I was facing it. Unfortunately, a quick search of these areas turned up negative.*

After an unsuccessful all-day search for Bud on Saturday, including several trips to the Humane Society, I emailed Bill at his home in Virginia. He suggested that I scan a photo of Buddy, and email it to him along with a map link of my home address some 9,000 miles away in Hawaii!

On Monday morning, Bill sent me an email advising that Buddy was in an area that was south of my home, still hiding in some heavy brush, about a quarter mile away. Bud was lost and uncomfortable, but still alive. My friends and I spent over five hours combing this very difficult terrain within a three-quarter-mile radius, constantly calling for Buddy, hoping that he'd hear us and at least respond with a howl to let us know where he was. No luck.

Exhausted from hiking and attempting to navigate through the heavy brush, including overgrown California grass, kiawe, lantana, haole koa, etc., I decided to follow what the pig hunters do when they lose one or more of their hunting dogs: I tied my now very soiled shirt to a low-hanging branch near the entrance to the forest, hoping that Bud would pick up my scent, find the spot where I left my shirt, and wait for me to get him later that night or the next day. But still, no Bud.

On Tuesday morning, Bill sent me some grim emails to my office downtown. This was now the fifth day that Buddy had been gone. It seems that Bud was still in the same area as he was before, but emitting a much lower energy level. Bill suggested that the dog may have been attacked by other dogs or wild pigs overnight, and that if it was Buddy's destiny to leave this world, we should hope that he passed quickly and without much suffering. I immediately phoned the bad news on to my friends. Hoping to save the dog, they began yet another frantic search of the area suggested by Bill. No luck.

Frustrated and more depressed while at work, I called and spoke directly with Bill in Virginia the same afternoon. He suggested that the low energy readings of Buddy could be indicative of the dog simply resting. Buddy was still in the same area, but without much longer to live.

Sensing my desperation, Bill agreed to conduct another reading of Bud's whereabouts while we were on the phone. Attempting to be more exact, he placed a red dot marked by an arrow, pinpointing the spot on map where the dog would be. Bill then scanned the map and emailed it to me. Then Bill asked, "Do you believe in angels?" If I did, then I should ask my angels for assistance in finding Buddy. Whatever skepticism I now had about animal psychics, spirituality extending to animals, and so forth, was being put to the test.

Bill then suggested that I follow some tips on locating Buddy using dowsing rods, or "divining rods." Most important, he said, I had to trust my spiritual self and not be bashful about asking my angels for assistance.

Understand, while I am somewhat of a religious person in the sense that I believe in God, a Higher Being, I don't consider myself particularly holy or spiritually gifted in any special way.

Anxious, if not desperate, to get home to find my lost dog before he died, I finally made it home through pau hana traffic around 5 p.m. With not much more time to spare before losing sunlight, I fabricated two makeshift dowsing rods according to Bill's specs using two wire clothes hangers.

I then proceeded to walk the edge of my neighborhood where I had tied my shirt the day before. With one wire hanger in each hand, I placed my trust in Bill's advice and asked my angels to guide me to my lost dog. Rather than frantically calling for Buddy as my friends and I had done on prior occasions, I tried a different and more subdued approach to coax him to come out from the bushes, assuming that he was not injured, only scared. Admittedly, I was concerned my neighbors would see me with two wire hangers in hand yelling for my dog and think I had finally gone over the edge. But I calmly let Buddy know I was searching for him, and assured him I was going to find him.

The technique worked! Within half an hour of when I had started following my dowsing sticks that took me exactly to the point on the map that Bill had marked, the hangers started twirling in circles like the arrow in a compass after you shake it. Instead of returning in the direction that it had been leading me, the hangers were turned in almost the opposite direction, now pointing toward my home! It was quite odd. I thought maybe that it was the wind, so I faced in the direction of my home, expecting the hangers to return to the original direction that they were leading me. They did not, at least not immediately. Gradually, the hangers began pointing in a direction that would cause me to start heading back to where I had started – by the tree where I had tied my shirt.

At that point, because it was getting dark, I called my friend, Curtis to let him know where I was just in case I got lost. His cell phone was busy, so I left a message. About 15 minutes later, while still attempting to navigate my way out of the thick brush and trees and losing sunlight fast, I received an ecstatic call from Curtis that Bud had just run up my driveway to my garage!

I know for certain that my angels were right on the money when the direction of my hangers abruptly changed from the direction that they were leading me, and instead pointing me in the direction of my house. Bill's reading of where Bud was hiding from Thursday's thunderstorm was correct all along, unchanged from when he first provided a reading to my mother when he was still in Hawaii.

Believe me, I am no longer a skeptic. Thanks to Bill Northern, Buddy and I are happily reunited! Amen.

Robert Chong, Esquire
Honolulu, Hawaii
March 2004

The Healing Journals

The late Harold McCoy is pictured here at The Ozark Research Institute.

Dowsing for Healing

Cliff Sanderson was the first dowser to tell me dowsing could be used in healing. He was from New Zealand and I met him in 1994 at the American Society of Dowsers (ASD) convention in Lyndonville, Vermont. He told us how you could put your hands on somebody and heal them, much like faith healers do. Cliff told us the most important thing was good intent. With good intent, you can put your hands on someone and just ask God to heal them and it will happen. I think the ASD did not talk about healing out of concern of being sued by doctors. I'm not sure.

But I wanted to know more. So in 1995, I went to a healing class taught by the renowned Harold McCoy. I had heard him speak about dowsing at the same ASD convention.

He had taken dowsing principles into healing. He went on to establish a research organization called The Ozark Research Institute. Today, the state of Arkansas charters them as a non-profit to train people and research into the "Power of Thought." Their particular inquiry into the Power of Thought is how it might create miraculous healing, remission, and other health recovery methods.

Back then, Harold would rent a Methodist retreat center and hold a healing and training session. There were 100 students, five healers. Students were divided into five classrooms of 20 students each. The healers spent a day with each group and taught their particular method of healing.

Bill Meets His Angels

Harold taught us about how to tune into your spirit guides or angels, and how to tell the difference. In those early years, Harold or one of his helpers would collect you at the airport and return you at the end of the week. At the end of my training, Harold's son drove us back to the airport. In the car, he asked me if I'd learned a lot that week.

"I don't know if I should say this, but I did not learn much from your dad," I said. A young lady in the back asked why. "I wasn't able to relate to the tools he used, I think."

She leaned forward. "What do you do for a living?" she asked. I told her I sold janitor supplies. Then she asked if I had good brushes, brooms, and cleaners.

"Of course!" I said. "Wardico is very successful with a wide assortment of products."

"Well, why don't you use some of those items? Ones you're familiar with?"

This was a great point! And it was what I needed to hear. Harold and Cliff – and in some way, that young woman for making that point – would become my best teachers.

Bill Gets Help from His Angels

I went to work fixing peoples' backs. I did all of my work at night. Just as Harold taught, I mentally unzipped the skin over the vertebrae and envisioned the back to examine it. I could usually see the problem and I used items I was familiar with to fix it. I mentally used silicone and epoxy with great success on the vertebrae.

For lungs, I envisioned using the tips of feathers to remove tar caused by smoking. I would first mentally picture myself using cleaners to soften the tar, then the feathers could remove it.

When I told my longtime friend and horse client Dave Wheeler about attending Harold's class, he became one of my first healing clients. He was having difficulty breathing. I mentally cleaned his lungs but it only lasted four to six weeks. One night I awoke, and saw tiny hands sewing something in Dave's chest. I kept watching and realized they were Angels' hands sewing a healthy baby's lung in him. At first it did not seem very beneficial. But as the lung "grew," Dave was improving. His "new lung" lasted many years and is just now getting tired.

Dave was so happy with his healing experience, he began to study Neuro-Link, or Neural Integration Systems, along with Lucy Giles. They both were good and helped many people. Both have a nice following in New Zealand. Lucy had asked me to come over and work with some horses. When I arrived, she realized my neck bothered me and asked if she could fix it. She began to lightly tap in different areas on the top of my head. She told me this was the method Neuro-Link. Believe it or not, it worked! It took away my neck pain and the relief lasted between four and five days.

Renowned Horse Trainer
Gets Help From Bill & Wins Big

By Michael P. Leahy

General Manager of Wynsome Stables
As told to Cesca Janece Waterfield on January 20, 2022

When I was told what Bill did, I was very skeptical. But I had a horse named Suyeta that was having quite a number of issues in his training. I've always been the type of person to think outside the box. So I thought, well, if Bill could do what he said he could do, then I was willing to give it a try.

I'd had Suyeta under my care for six months. I picked him out of a barn when he was six months old. I had an innate feeling that he was a special horse. But he was really, really difficult for my employees and everything to work around. I had tried a lot of things with him. So this one employee introduced me to Bill as a horse communicator. I'd never met anybody like that before, but if he could help me with the horse, it would be a huge benefit to me and a benefit to the horse so I could understand what was wrong.

Bill said to me, "The only way this works, is if what Suyeta tells me, you follow through with."

I said, "Sure, I'll follow through. I really don't have another option. I've tried everything else."

Bill told me, "I'm gonna tell you what I find, and if you follow through, we'll be good."

He went and he dowsed the horse and he came back to me and he said, "Look, I need you to do two things for me. The horse has had a dislocated poll for six months. The person who had the horse before you had tied the horse to a wall and he pulled back off the wall and he dislocated his poll."

Bill said, "Make two phone calls. Under no circumstances tell any of the two people you call I was here. One, call a chiropractor. When the chiropractor is finished, she's going to tell you that you need a dentist because when the chiropractor realigns his poll, that's going to realign his teeth."

So that's what I did. I called the chiropractor and I had her look at five horses, not just him. After she had done two horses, she went to look at Suyeta and she called my attention. She said, "Do you realize this horse's poll has been dislocated for six months?

I said, "No, I didn't, but I do now." She said, "I'm going to put it back into place, but you need to call your dentist and have him come because Suyeta's teeth are going to need to be realigned."

So I did that within a week. I ran the horse in a race three weeks later. He won his first race going a mile by six lengths. That horse went on to win $250,000 and broke a track record at Keeneland. I had him up until two years ago. I gave him a home and then I buried him in my front yard. I had him from the time he was a baby. That was the first introduction I had to Bill Northern. The whole deal with Suyeta knocked it home for him. Because there was no way he could know what he knew. I'd never met the man before and he'd never met those horses before.

Astonished in Kentucky

The next experience with Bill that was amazing to me was a real, real special horse. This was something that took me a long time to even get my head around. The horse's name was Freedom Alert. He had gotten injured and I had met Bill at a horse sale in Lexington, Kentucky. Now this horse Freedom Alert was an hour and twenty minutes away in Cincinnati. I was really concerned because a number of vets told me this horse would never race. One vet told me the horse needed to be put down. I met Bill at the sale and he said, "Is everything okay?"

I said, "No, I'm in trouble with one of the horses. I'm really concerned about him."

But we were in Lexington at the time. He said, "Look, I'm going to do something and I don't do it too often. But I'm going to show you what I can do." I said, "Okay."

We were at a sale and there were a number of horses in front of us. He said, "Now watch. I'm going to take the horse standing in front of me and I'm going to substitute that horse for Freedom Alert. So I'm going turn the horse in front of me into Freedom Alert for five minutes so I can diagnose what's wrong with Freedom Alert."

Now Freedom Alert was an hour and twenty minutes away. But the minute Bill said that, that horse showed the problems in his leg—he showed the lameness that Freedom Alert had. He went lame on the leg Freedom Alert was lame in. There was no way Bill could know that. I didn't tell him anything. I just told him I was concerned about a horse that was an hour and twenty minutes away. Immediately, the minute he said, "I'm going to substitute this horse for Freedom Alert," that horse in front walked off lame in his left front leg.

So I asked Bill, "What do I do?" He said, "Don't listen to anybody. You keep doing what you're doing and that horse will come around. That horse will run through fire for you and nobody else."

I got the horse back and I ran him in a race. He didn't

win the race but he did okay. Both Suyeta and Freedom Alert
are buried alongside each other in my front yard.

Communicating with the Mare

The third one was a mare. She was highly strung and I
was having trouble with the horse. The day Bill dowsed
Suyeta, I told him I had another one. He couldn't see her feet
because she was standing in two foot of straw. But he said,
"Number one, you've changed her shoes last week," which I
had. He said, "She doesn't like her shoes. You need to change
them back to the way you had them. Secondly, she doesn't like
surprises. You need to tell her everyday for seven days before
she races how you want her to race and where she's going to
be running. Tell her then, at night when you have quality time
with the horses."

That's quality time with me and my horses when
there's nobody around. I'm there at 4 o'clock in the morning
but there's people there. But at 6 or 7 o'clock at night,
everybody's gone home and it's just me and the horses. Bill
was able to tell me that the horses knew that's when we had

quality time. So I would go in and tell her how I wanted her to run and where she was going to run. Just standing at the end of the day. I'd walk through all the horses to see how they were doing. I'd just come up to her stall and say, "Listen, you need to break out of the gate and sit at second or third and don't get intimidated by the other horses. The jockey's going to lead you through, and just put your best race forward."

That's what she did. She came out three weeks later and ran the best race of her life. Now she didn't win, but she ran the best race she'd ever ran of her life. And this is all off what he told me to do.

Entering The Northern Arena at The Virginia Horse Center Foundation in Lexington, Virginia.

The Virginia Horse Center Names The Northern Arena for Bill

On October 29, 2011, The Virginia Horse Center Foundation in Lexington, Virginia, dedicated an arena to Bill, naming it the Northern Arena. Hoofbeats Therapeutic Riding

Program performed, and Pastor William M. Klein of Lexington Presbyterian Church conducted a blessing of the animals. Naturally, all animals were welcome at the ceremony, and a reception celebrated the event at The Winner's Ring. The following week, the event was reported in Lexington's newspaper the *News-Gazette*.

Remarks by Katherine Truitt
Executive Director, Virginia Horse Center Foundation, October 29, 2011

Thank you for joining us on this chilly afternoon to applaud a very good friend of ours and oversee the formal dedication of the Northern Arena. Before I begin, I want to thank Pastor Klein for being with us today and for conducting a wonderful animal blessing, and our Hoofbeats riders for offering their time even though scheduling conflicts and the weather got in the way this time. I am so glad that the Trials riders are using and enjoying the Northern Arena today though.

Bill Northern is a renowned dowser and animal communicator, well known for his talents in this industry. He has helped countless animals and owners find resolution and bridge the gap where words failed. In a similar spirit, Bill has made a gift of support to the Virginia Horse Center Foundation that will help us extend ourselves to meet the needs of our exhibitors, the community, and the state of Virginia. On behalf of the Board of Directors and the staff, I offer deep and heartfelt thanks for the resources and friendship Bill has provided.

One of the best parts of being involved here is getting to interact with astonishing individuals like Bill Northern. So many talented people come through our gates but it is rare that someone returns to reward a facility it deems worthy. I am humbled at Bill's vote of confidence and gladdened by his friendship. The Virginia Horse Center Foundation is about to embark on the next 25 years with the help of a hard working staff and board of directors, with talented riders like some of you today, with community members dedicated to helping the

Center succeed, and the help of invaluable partners like you, Bill.

I welcome everyone to explore the sign outside and enjoy the horse show on grounds, the Virginia Horse Trials. I will now invite Christine Drake to introduce Pastor William Klein who will conduct an animal blessing!

Animal Communication in Hawaii

The trip of December 2013 through February 2014 was a very rewarding trip. With Delta sending me pre-checked through security, the trip was off to a great start. We were able to assist a great number of clients with their animal issues and also teach some people who will carry on our work in years to come.

I arrived in Hawaii the first part of December and was collected at the airport by my friend and student David Baba. David has been working with both animals and energy fields. Every year he gains more confidence in his dowsing.

Cindy Comer organizes my schedule while I am in Hawaii. She is most efficient and does a great job. Cindy also does energy work with animals and sells nutritional supplements for people and animals. She is knowledgeable and takes her work seriously. As usual, I stayed at A-Tri-K Stables in Waimanalo. My usual host Wayne Shizuru was in California so I was on my own.

My first animal communication client planned to take lessons later. Her two dogs, Ace and Biscuit, were fun to work with. The younger dog, Biscuit, wanted to see the horses. So at the end of the session we walked both dogs down the aisle to see the horses. When Ace first saw a horse put her head down to greet him, he wanted to leave. He didn't want anything to do with something this big.

Talk to Your Pets

The next day's item of interest was a Brittany Spaniel named Ranger. The owner Rob said Ranger would not come to him when called. I told Rob I wasn't a dog trainer and he could leave without owing me anything. He decided to stay and it turned out I was able to help. Ranger communicated to me, *I don't come because he often calls me just as I'm smelling the quail. I'm exploring! It's very inconvenient to stop and come at his whim.*

I explained to Robert what Ranger had communicated. I recommended that he talk to Ranger each time and explain why he needed to come when called, even if not convenient. When I bumped into Rob a few weeks later, he said Ranger had really improved in coming when called.

"Uncle Bill has helped me and my animals tremendously; so many times, I can't even begin to count," says Chantal Lactaoen, pictured here.

'Uncle Bill' & His Angels

I've had the honor and privilege to know Uncle Bill for the past 17 years. In Hawaii, out of respect, the elders are either Uncle, Aunty, Tutu, or Papa. We are one big Ohana, which means family. Uncle Bill has helped me and my animals tremendously, so many times that I can't even begin to count.

Koa, my first horse, nearly broke my spirit. He was "green" and so was I. I had no knowledge or experience. I've just always loved animals and have always wanted a horse since I was a child. I thought, finally, at the age of 37 when I got my first horse, it would be everything I've always dreamed of . . . not! Instead, I came home from the ranch crying on a daily basis.

But then I met Uncle Bill. When Uncle Bill walked up to Koa and I, the first thing that came out of his mouth was, "Are you sure you are going to keep him? He isn't patient in wanting to teach you how to ride."

I was very determined and told him yes. Throughout the couple years I had Koa, Uncle Bill helped me understand what Koa was thinking, and he helped me find an old-time cowboy who could help the two of us create an unconditional bond that I've always dreamed of. He was able to allow me to see and hear Koa's voice, know what was going on internally, where he was sore, how my riding and saddle affected him, etc. What Uncle Bill communicated was priceless.

My horse Play was a totally different story. The first thing Uncle Bill said to me as he walked up was, "You both are a match made in heaven." Music to my ears, it totally melted my heart! I remember when I had a child, Chalet, she was still in diapers walking around the stall with Play. Uncle Bill could not even communicate with Play, he was so concerned about Chalet and her safety! Uncle Bill told me I would never have to worry about Play around Chalet and that Play would always look after and protect her. To this day, he is still so gentle and careful around Chalet and any child that is near him. With Uncle Bill and his Angels' ability to communicate to us what our horses are feeling, thinking, and saying, it has been the most incredible journey that I've ever experienced with my horses. It has allowed me to be one with them as well as solidified this incredible bond, something I've always dreamed of since I was a child.

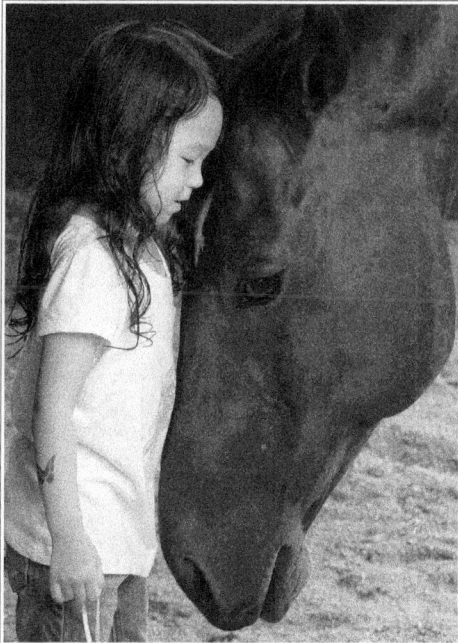

*Chalet stands with her mother's
horse, Play.*

*Words can't even begin to express my complete
gratitude to Uncle Bill for allowing me this precious gift of
being able to bond with my horses. Love you, Uncle Bill!*

Chantal Lactaoen
Kahalu'u, Oahu, Hawaii

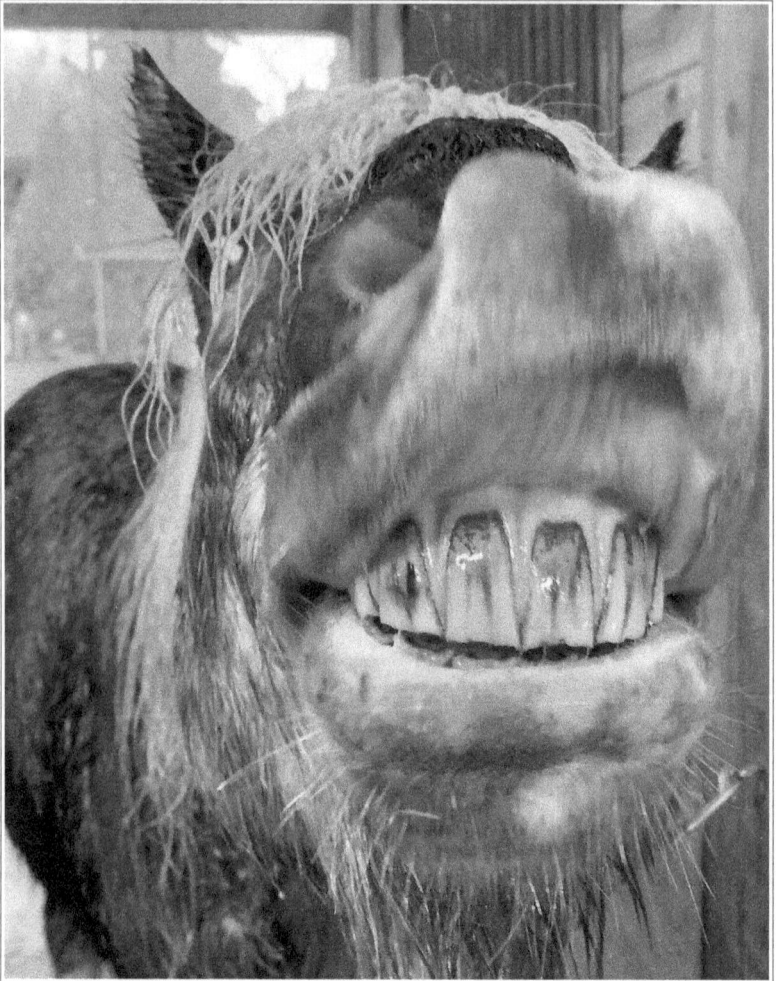

This smiling fella is Loki, Natasha Chornesky's handsome horse.

A Hoof Infection Cured

Bill, Just checking in to let you know we are well past a year since Loki, my horse, spoke with you. We are a much stronger team now, stronger than ever. Based on what Loki shared with you, we were able to find a center sulcus infection in the hoof about which the two of you spoke. In fact, we treated all four hooves and increased his copper and zinc to offset hay that is too high in iron. As for his upset tummy, that turned out to be hind gut ulcers. Once I [changed trainers], his condition dramatically improved. He's been steady for months now.

The biggest difference has been in how much more communicating I do with Loki. Per your recommendation, I always keep Loki informed of daily and weekly plans. I greet him in the morning and review the day's activities. When I say goodnight, I always tell him what's in store for the next day.

Thank you again for all your help. Stay safe and healthy. God bless!

Loki and Natasha Chornesky, Ed.M.

Helping Ann Heal

Near the end of December I shifted up to Rolleston, New Zealand, to be with my friend Ann Butts who I normally stay with when in the area. Rolleston is the largest town in the Selwyn District of New Zealand, and it's central to most of the farms where I have clients.

But Ann was having some health complications and she wasn't doing well. She told me she's tired and that she's just ready to pass away, she's tired of fighting. On New Year's Eve, her son Dave took her to the hospital. She asked if I could watch her dog, Mishka. I let her know I didn't mind and that I'll be right over. I now needed to stay there and look after the house. Ann is fortunate that two of her granddaughters work at the hospital where she is a patient. One is a nurse and the other is in radiation. They are able to see her regularly and it means a lot to her for them to call in. The doctors still do not know what is wrong with her. Her son showed me how to use the TV to watch the daily horse races. I have clients that go all over the country racing. It's nice to be able to watch them. The next day, Dave Wheeler and his wife Hazel, who is a good cook, brought me a nice salmon lunch. Recently, Dave started teaching Hazel Neuro-Link. More on that later.

Mishka does not like to walk with me. So in order to give her exercise, I break bread in very small pieces and place them on the leaves of shrubbery around the yard. With the constant wind in New Zealand, some pieces blow off. She walks around the yard several times to locate all of them. She doesn't want the birds to find her food.

Dave is sending out a community text messages every day relating to Ann's condition. It seems that the doctors are running many tests but are unable to come up with a definite diagnosis. Dave Wheeler, Lester Morris, and I are checking with her every day and we agree the problem is with her heart.

The doctors think her heart is over-worked because of other health issues.

On Monday the 13th of January, the report was about the same from Ann. I remembered something we learned from the healing school at The Ozark Research Institute in Fayetteville, Arkansas. Harold McCoy taught that there were points in the ears and feet that connected to different organs in the body. So I mentally placed needles in Ann's big toes and ears. Then I connected the needles with wires which were connected to a 9-volt battery. This was to give her enough energy to help her heal whatever needed to. The next day she was a bit better, but then the battery went flat. So I mentally pictured a larger battery and connected the wires. This battery was a bit too strong as she was shaky. So I visualized a battery connected to a transformer where I could control the voltage flow. This was exactly what she needed and she responded nicely.

Ann's 17th Day in the Hospital

She is now improving a bit each day. I adjusted her

energy level as it was a bit high again. I got a text from Dave telling me Ann may be able to come home the following day. I went home and filled her car with petrol, washed the car, vacuumed the carpet, and did a general house cleaning. I wanted everything to be right for Ann when she came home. She rang me the next morning to tell me that she needed to prove to the hospital that she was capable of living alone so I would need to find somewhere else to live. I had not considered this. I had about two hours to find another place to stay. I first rang Tyrone as he keeps a room for me whenever I am in New Zealand. He has a large five bedroom house and used to rent rooms. Now the spare rooms just collect outdated electronic equipment. He suggested Dave bring me to Rakaia as he was very busy. Tyrone now has two Mobil stations to look after and he's on the board of directors of a couple organizations, so he travels a lot. Dave took me to Rakaia after he brought Ann home. She does not look well and can barely walk with a walker. But she really does need to be home. After all, she has been in a hospital bed for 24 days, mostly in intensive care.

It was good to be able to stay with Tyrone, as Rakaia is in the range of most of my clients but his house is generally cold. A lot of Kiwis are tough and actually like the cold. Many wear shorts and a tee shirt when it is 50 - 55 Farenheit degrees outside. Tyrone is one of them. Shortly after I got settled at Tyrone's, Michael and Pauline Ward rang and said they were happy to have me come and stay at their house for a fortnight. This was a dream come true as I have known them for years. Besides, Pauline is one of the best cooks anywhere. They have a couple of young horses that are not training to their potential, so this is a good opportunity for me to help.

Radionics &
Illness in Horses

On my way to Christchurch, New Zealand, I stopped over in Auckland and stayed with my friends, Alistair Cox and Jenneane Sowry. Alistair and Jenneane also work with animals. However, rather than communication, they're concerned with diagnosing sickness and illness, primarily in horses. They look for lameness and recommend homeopathic remedies for the horses, and they're good at it.

I arrived on a Sunday and they had a lot of folks come over that were interested in healing and different metaphysical phenomena. Jenneane put on a really good feed for everybody that had guests coming and going.

Then on Monday, Alistair needed to go out to the Thoroughbred Training Center outside of Auckland at

Pukekohe Park to collect a couple of saliva samples from horses, bring them back, and review them. Alistair and Jenneane use radionics machines for analysis. Each of them has their own machine that they use for diagnosis. *Editor's Note: For more in-depth information on radionics, see the Appendix of this book.* The type of radionics machine that Alistair and Jenneane have has two probes and a specimen chamber where a saliva sample goes. As you move the probe over a horse, the machine will beep when you get to a place on the horse that's sore. For suspected internal problems with heart, liver, lungs, etc., they just touch these areas with the probe, and the machine beeps if there's a problem. Alistair and Jenneane also have a long list of questions about the horse's diet, whether it's been exposed to pesticides, insecticides, and so forth. If the horse is positive for any of those, the machine will beep to let them know.

Now you can laugh at this, and it's true you won't find many of these machines in the United States because some radionics units have been banned here. According to the government, there's nothing in this machine that actually works as claimed. But I've seen radionics machines used accurately and successfully! Just don't go running out thinking you're going to buy one easily in the U.S. today.

Alistair and I stopped at the Thoroughbred Training Center to get saliva samples so Alistair and Jenneane could diagnose the horses. The trainer wasn't there but the assistant trainer told us to go ahead and see the horses and the trainer would catch up with us.

The first horse we looked at was a little filly, two years old. Alistair got a saliva sample from her which was easy. To get a sample, he takes a dab of litmus paper and sticks it on a horse's tongue. She was willing to communicate and told me right away where she hurt. She had a lot of aches and pains. She was not accustomed to all this hard work, and she wasn't happy with it. She told me her rider had hit her twice that morning. She wasn't pleased with her jockey.

We went to see the next horse and he was standing in shavings. For bedding in the United States, we use a lot of straw. In New Zealand, they use mostly wood shavings. This horse was standing in wood shavings so deep you could barely see his hooves. Alistair got a sample from him, and asked me to see what I could learn about this horse because they had been having some problems with him. I went over the horse and found places he said he was sore. The horse communicated to me that his hooves were the reason for the problem. He said his right front hoof wasn't level and it really should be. Then he communicated to me that his left front hoof should be high on the inside. Instead, they had it lower on the inside. I went over his hooves and his left hind leg had a defect, what we call a confirmation problem. On the right side, his hoof didn't grow into heel. The horse communicated that he needed more heel on that hoof to have enough support.

The assistant trainer came along and we relayed to him what we had heard from both horses. He couldn't believe that the little two-year-old filly had told us about his rider that morning. He admitted the rider had cracked her twice with the whip because she wasn't doing what the rider wanted her to do.

We told the trainer where the other horse had said he was sore. The trainer was amazed when we told him about the problems with the hooves on this particular horse, when the horse was standing so deep in shavings that you could hardly see them. But we'd been able to tell which hoof was level and which wasn't. We knew which was too high, which was too low, and amazingly, about the right hind leg not getting enough support.

Later, when Alistair went over these horses using his radionics machine, he found virtually the same problems that we had found earlier in person. With the help of Alistair and my Angels, we were able to get this little two-year-old filly to where she felt better and wasn't complaining as much, and they were able to get the older horse balanced again so he could race well. I don't know if he won his next race, but he was much better, and his trainers and owner were pleased.

A Christmas Gift of Healing

My husband Andy and I first met Bill in 2001. I decided that for Christmas, I wanted Bill to come and talk with our horses. While Andy was skeptical, I met the moment with quiet anticipation of unlocking doors to my horses' minds. I was not disappointed in the least.

Bill first talked with Sadie. She is a three-year-old Morgan mare who was diagnosed with Equine Protozoal Myeloencephalitis. She has a right hind deficiency that I wanted Bill to evaluate. The first thing that Bill said was that Sadie was very eager to have me know something about her. A spot on her spinal column had been injured due to some acupuncture work. Sadie wanted me to know about this. I had suspected some problems in this area as she had a very distinctive reaction to the therapy. Bill immediately pointed to the exact area on her spine where the needles had been inserted. He proceeded to tell me that Sadie wanted me to know that she had been hurt there. The EPM was gone, and other than some physical therapy and gradual buildup of activity, Sadie was just fine. It was so nice to know that my concerns and thoughts about her were confirmed.

Next came Ginny. She had repetitive bouts of colic over the past year. It was always mild, yet a constant source of concern for us. Bill, again, told us immediately that Ginny had a very upset stomach that was at the point of having an ulcer. He also noted a problem on her left kidney. He advised us on how to help her stomach problems. A year later, she had to be hospitalized for a severe high fever and, while there, the vet did an ultra sound on her. Much to my shock, the results of the scan revealed a 50mm cyst on her left kidney. Bill's findings were confirmed again.

Neither of these horses had any inkling that Bill was coming, nor had he been prepped with any information that could lead to these discoveries while talking with them. Bill asked a few short questions of some of the other horses, and we laughed at their responses. It was as if they were coming "directly" from the horses' mouths on several key issues. I was excited to tell Andy that night of Bill's visit and all that he had learned from our horses. Andy was convinced that I must have been talking Bill's head off, and gave away the things that Bill had learned.

So I arranged for Bill to return and talk with our stallion with Andy present. Andy had a long-time problem in getting Virgil to track to the left while in harness. The horse just refused to bend to the shafts properly. Bill told us that Virgil had relayed to him that an accident had happened to him while at the trainer that was a pivotal changing point in his way of going. He had taken a fall and had some damage to the right hind end. It made sense.

But Virgil was not through with Bill. He said that he had a concern about Andy's hearing. It seems as though Andy was always raising his voice to him so he assumed that Andy had a hearing problem. I howled with laughter as Bill told us this as I could just see Virgil saying this with tongue-in-cheek sarcasm. Andy just simply yelled a lot at the horse, and Virgil was diplomatically letting us know that the loud voice was not really necessary.

The most amazing part of Virgil's talk with Bill came next. As I stated earlier, Virgil did not like bending into the shafts going one direction. Andy was determined to fix this problem, and worked to that end. Driving him along fences and the curved exterior of our round pen was the training tool for Virgil in an attempt to get him to bend properly. The next comment from our horse was that he was also concerned about Andy's vision. He stated that Andy had a tendency to drive too close to the fencing, and, in fact, had driven the shafts through the fence boards one day when he cut it a bit too close. This is precisely what had happened, as I saw it myself months earlier. Bill did not know about this episode, but Virgil was most adamant that this was a problem. He was right.

I could go on and on with anecdotal tales about Bill and horses of mine and others. I have sent people to him from all over the country, and in fact, Andy and I have taken his dowsing class to learn how to talk with animals. It seemed so very easy that I could not believe it was as simple as it seemed. Bill stressed lots of practice to both Andy and me, and it is now paying off. I have been very fortunate that my own angels have enabled me to talk to several horses so far. I have made sure that the information I received was reliable and verifiable. Glad to say that through Bill's tutelage, I am now able to talk with horses of several friends very easily.

Bill has opened up a whole new world for us with his guidance, support and help. I cannot say enough wonderful things about him that could possibly do him justice. He is a very kindhearted soul and in the truest sense, a "gentle man." I count myself most fortunate that Bill Northern has crossed our path.

Darcy & Andy Donahue
June 2003

The Cosmic Bettie Cox

Each time I spoke with Bettie it was an adventure. She first contacted me to go over her horses remotely. I didn't know her at the time, but several of my clients had recommended me to her. In her late fifties then, she was an accomplished rodeo rider who competed for buckles, but mainly money. She was the only person I knew that put a lot of faith in the zodiac. She would even pick friends born in a sign compatible to her. She did the same for animals. She only bought horses that were born under the right zodiac sign. Bettie had four horses and she knew each one's birthday.

Bettie had a great intuition. Yes, when she called me she wanted to know what was wrong with her animals, but she would already have an idea. The call to me was just to find *exact* information. For example, horses need to be wormed every few months and there are several medicines to use. So she would call me to ask which medicines to use, and when to use them.

Helping the Four-Legged Family

Bettie contacted me when her little turtle Clyde stopped eating. I communicated with Clyde remotely and he showed me what he wanted to eat. Years later, that turtle is still alive. Clyde spends most of his time in the barn, but sometimes she brings him in the house. Bettie also had a cat she loved dearly. One afternoon she called to tell me Apollo was in the hospital and the vet didn't know what the trouble was. So I remotely reached out to Apollo. He showed me that he'd eaten a mouse that had been poisoned. When Bettie told the vet what I'd learned, he knew what antidote to give Apollo.

Bettie's husband Jim was in construction. One day I visited them in Waikiki where he was building a huge home with a swimming pool. Though I knew Jim, my contact with the couple was exclusively through Bettie.

Bettie was quite generous. She took me to lunch at least once a year, setting the dates according to the zodiac. She liked restaurants with valet parking. She would always tip the valet $10, tip the waiter at least $20, then tip the valet who returned her car another $10. Needless to say, everyone at the restaurant was very pleased to see her come in.

One day Bettie called and said God told her and Jim to move to California but He did not tell them where. They asked me to pick out the town where they were supposed to move. I printed out a map and looked over the whole state to find the perfect place: the eastern part of the state. Jim looked over properties for sale and chose five with suitable farms. He flew out to look at them in person, narrowing them down to two. Then he asked me which should they buy. I chose one that happened not to have a barn on it, but that was no problem for Jim. He knew he could build one himself. They negotiated the price and brought it.

Bettie soon became friends with people in the area,

especially those with quarter horses. She continued to call me, mostly to confirm decisions she had made. She would ask about all sorts of things – if she should attend the horse show this weekend, and if so, which horses she should take. She was always relying on the zodiac, but checked with me to make sure she was right.

When some years later Jim had a heart attack and passed away, I found out that he had been the one who initially told Bettie to contact me. That surprised me, but it was reassuring.

One thing about Bettie and Jim: At night they watched old Westerns with a bottle of Champagne. They would eat, drink, enjoy the Westerns, and go to sleep. It's very seldom you meet couples like that.

Lights in a Difficult Time

Hi Bill, We met back in the late 90s. My husband had recently died. A few weeks after he died, a mockingbird began knocking on a window of the house every morning. No matter which room I was in, he would find me and peck at the glass until he got my attention. Sometimes he would actually crash-land if I didn't hear him! You talked to him and told me he had lost his mate, too, and knew that I was hurting. He wanted me to come outside and see his new home, that he had sorta fallen in love with me. So very touching and sweet. I ended up losing the home and property to unscrupulous lawyers and traveled out west for the next 12 years. Two years ago I moved to Richmond and started a Reiki practice, which has extended to animals. Imagine my surprise when a client asked if I had ever heard of Bill Northern! You talked to her horse, Landon. It brought back wonderful memories, lights during a difficult time. Just popping in to say hello and let you know you made a wonderful difference! Thank you.

Mary
Richmond, Virginia

Kimberly Jungherr stands with her Holsteiner horse, Conte Couleur.

Bill's Journal: Back in the Ring

Monday, March 5, 2018

Saturday was the best day I have had in a long time. I came to Florida in late January with the thought of attending the HITS Winter Circuit Horse Show. HITS is a company that produces hunter and jumper horse shows. I'd been to a HITS show in Culpeper, Virginia, and had many friends who went. However, I was leery about attending the Florida show for the first time because, not being able to walk very far, I would have to rent a golf cart and I didn't know where any golf cart rentals were. Then I began to think I wouldn't know anyone there because in looking at the results online, I didn't see any names I recognized. On top of that, I didn't know anyone in the town of Williston interested in the show to drive me. Finally, I just decided not to go.

But on Friday night I rang my neighbor Larry and

asked if he would drive me to the horse show the next day. I suggested we rent a golf cart and only stay two hours. Larry agreed.

He came to collect me at 10 a.m. wearing his best Western attire. We located a golf cart rental. I was glad Larry was driving because as we tried to get through the HITS storage area to pick up the cart, Larry had to use some nice reverse driving skill to get us out, as a worker advised us there were probably nails on the pavement ahead.

At last we got our cart and drove around the tents looking for someone I knew. I saw no one. We went to jumper ring two and watched some horses. Larry had never been to a jumping show, so I explained the scoring to him. That's when he began to enjoy it. The class ended and I still hadn't seen a familiar face. For me, it's just not much fun hearing the horses trying to overcome being sore somewhere and trying to balance their unbalanced riders yet having no one for me to tell their troubles to.

I thought we may as well watch a little of the next class

before venturing over to watch riders in the hunter ring. That's when I saw my old friend Aaron Vale and spoke to him briefly.

Then the day got really fun. The third rider happened to be my old friend Harold Chopping. I caught up to him just as the groom was taking his horse back to the barn. For a moment he didn't recognize me. But then he exclaimed my name. Harold reminded me of the time at the HITS Show in Culpeper when they had a water shortage and were hauling in several truck loads of water daily. At that show, I had given Harold, Todd Minikas, and two others dowsing rods and we all went looking for good potable drinking water to fill the needs of the show grounds. Harold said he would never forget seeing all five of us with our dowsing rods crossing at the same time and all in line. They later drilled a well on this vein of water and had all the water they needed. That was a great memory.

Larry and I then went over to watch some hunters. I tried to explain why judging the hunters was so hard because it is subjective. But I'm sure I didn't do a very good job as I do not understand the judging myself.

Next we went over to the tents looking for Starlite Stable where I knew I'd find Mark and Kim Jungherr. We found the stable. But Carla, a nurse working for the day as a groom, said Kim was off judging at another show while Mark was over at the stadium ring. I asked her to tell Kim and Mark I was by. When I gave her my name, her bright eyes became even brighter. She asked if I would speak to one of their horses.

Just what I'd hoped! I was wishing for this, because even though I had been doing remote readings the past two years, mostly for clients in New Zealand, Hawaii, and California, I had not actually touched a real horse in three years.

It was a real thrill to actually touch the horse standing in front of me and listen to his thoughts. I worked with three other horses after that one. As much as I love it, this work can be draining. I was worn out when Mark arrived. Carla told him about what the horses needed. We talked a bit. Mark said Kim was showing tomorrow but I told him I would not make it. She will call me next week.

Larry and I turned in our golf cart and headed back to Williston, where his wife Carol had a nice box lunch for me. Larry took me home, I ate my lunch, sat in my recliner, and slept for three hours.

It was a very good day.

Further Insight:
Appendix

DIVINING GUIDANCE

Healing with the Power
of the Focused Mind

By Gladys McCoy

The Ozark Research Institute
As told to Cesca Janece Waterfield on April 14, 2022

Harold's philosophy was that nothing ever happens in the body unless it starts in your mind first. Therefore, you have to find the place in the mind. When he started doing the meditations, he found that he could look inside the brain and see, he called them "ribbons." That was the trauma that was attached to an event in the body. The brain has no place to store trauma. It can store memories, but it has no place for trauma. So the trauma would get so strong in the brain, there was no room for it. So it would send it to the weakest part in

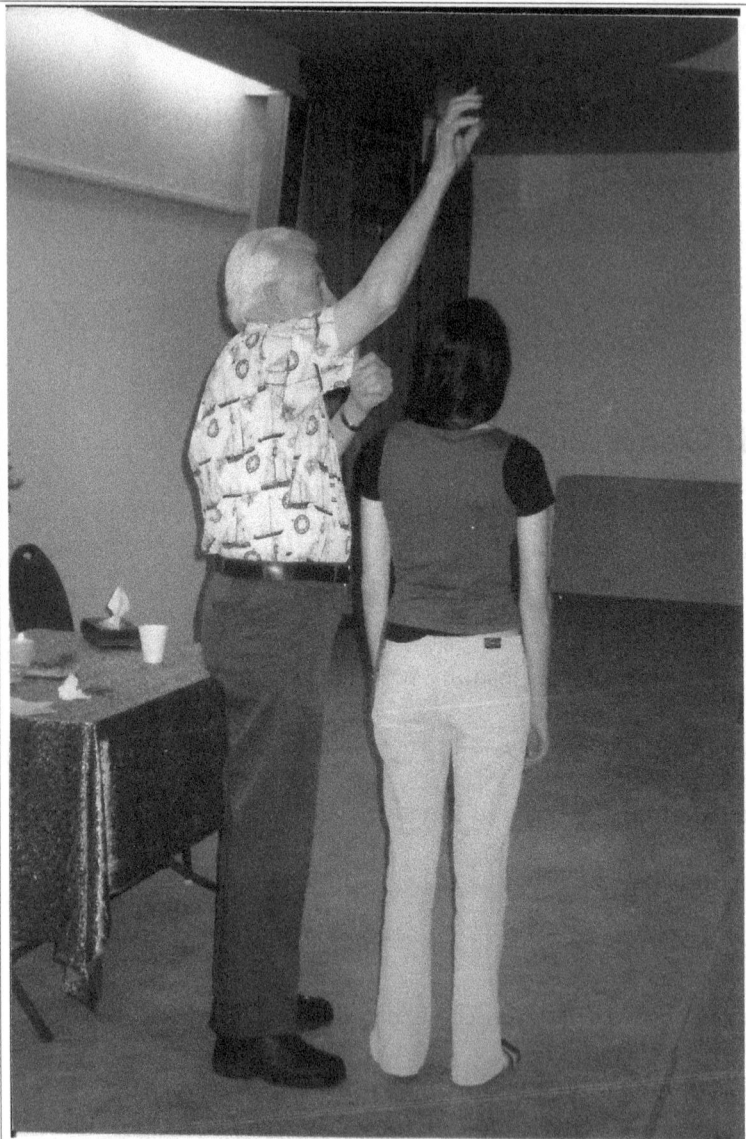

Founder of Ozark Research Institute and past President of the American Society of Dowsers, Harold McCoy taught that anyone could learn to heal others with love, and a focused mind in meditation.

the body. Wherever there was dis-ease or discomfort in the body, that's where it would go.

That's what he perceived when he first started doing the remote healing work. He was a dowser and he started with the dowsing. But he knew there was a connection that was much stronger than just that rod going down and pointing to the water in the ground. He believed there was a divine connection. As he worked with that, this healing started flowing in and he started doing the healing work with meditation.

That's what he perceived and it was all done with love. The longer he did it, the stronger it got. The last class he gave was in China, in Taiwan, and I think there were about 4,000 people in that room. It was 12 years ago that he had that last class in China. He taught people all over the world how to do this work. He wasn't unique in what he did. It was a "knowing" that he had. He had no training in anatomy, but he seemed to know a lot about anatomy when he started doing this. He said it was a knowing that would come to him. He said it was like going to your refrigerator and opening the door and you know where the milk is; you can just reach in and get it with your eyes closed. That's what he felt with the healing.

He started doing this work over 30 years ago. He would sit down every day, twice a day, and he would be in meditation for at least an hour. But he said he was always alert. He always knew what was going on around him. He could come out of meditation and go right back into the work again. He worked on thousands of people, hands-on as well as remote. The remote healing is very powerful because it's all done with love, and when you come from love, you can do no harm.

He did not diagnose and he did not prescribe. All during meditation, what he saw, he would manipulate the energy. He had these different techniques that came to him when a certain condition would come up. The book [*The Power of the Focused Mind]* we wrote about Harold describes what he did for autism, for brain tumors, for all these other things.

He was a very mechanical person. So most of the

healing he did was using mechanical things. He would actually be moving his hands. He'd reach in and gently "pull out" a tumor. One lady he taught, she was a cook, and she used a melon scoop. It was an imaginary thing, but he did it in meditation. It was real to him when he was doing it.

Anyone could do it. That was the miraculous thing about it. All you have to do is come with the desire to be of help to somebody else. That's what Harold always stressed, that he was nothing special. He tried to teach everybody in the class, how to do what he did, with stories of the healing work that he did. That's how he taught, was with stories.

I put the book together after Harold passed away. It was important to me that if the book went out, it had to be in Harold's words. Reading the book is just like hearing him talk. [After Harold died] I went to put papers away in his file cabinet. I noticed an envelope and there was a transcript of one of the workshops that he taught. That's what the book is. It's a teaching book. It tells you exactly what he did when he did the work on any dis-harmony that's going on in the body.

233

The book was put together as a workbook.

I don't know how it all works, but I do know that he worked really hard at it when he started doing it. He did a lot of good while he was on this earth plane and we believe he's still doing a lot of good for people. People call me and say, 'I know he was there. I know he showed me this.' I believe people that never met him have experienced his energy. He's just as busy now as he was when he was on this earth plane. And it's easier for him to travel around now.

'A Special Ability . . .
Which Everybody Has'

By Renton "Ren" Ellett

President, New Zealand Society for Dowsing and Radionics
As told to Cesca Janece Waterfield on April 1, 2022

Dowsing is the detection of the subtle energies of the earth and everything on it. Radionics is the manipulation of those energies for the benefit of the earth and everything on it. Radionics goes back to the early parts of the 20th century. They produced radionics boxes which were wires and dials and absolutely nothing in them. It puzzled me how people could do this. Then I got into radionics myself with an Atlantean Power Rod, which is a quartz crystal that resonates to me, with a tuned length of copper tube attached to it, blanked off on the end, wrapped in leather. I'm a dairy farmer, so my one idea was to attend to the fertility of the paddock, especially the trace elements that we seem to lack badly down here. That's where I sort of cut my teeth dowsing, was to figure out from soil tests and herbage tests what was lacking and how to dowse the soil. Then I moved into actually producing the energy of the required minerals to spread upon the paddocks. I got this from an Australian lady, Alana Moore, who's written a book, *Stone Age Farming.* She points out that this goes back way back in time. In England and Ireland, they had these round stone towers and nobody [contemporary] knew what they did. But [Moore says] that's what they were for, was the manufacturing and distribution of the energy of the minerals out on the paddocks. She modified this to a paramagnetic, rockdust-filled plastic tube put over a crossed energy point. So you need your dowsing skills to find the energy point, and that radiates the energy of the paramagnetic rockdust. That's where I'm coming from, but I've refined that.

I'm actually a skeptic with these things. It takes a lot of convincing me that they actually work, until they work on myself. I found a method that works for me.

I've been a dowser since 1990. Dowsing lends itself into various fields. You can do as I do, the agricultural. There's also the medical side too, which can get quite intriguing. Bill's a horse whisperer. I grew up with a father who was very much in tune with animals and I've worked with a dog whisperer. They're fascinating people, really. But they are using the principles and mind techniques of dowsing.

There's power in dowsing. You pick up an energy of something. You wander across the paddock with a pair of dowsing rods and you pick up all sorts of things, provided your mind is in the right direction, in the right frame of mind. I presume the horse whisperer and dog whisperer actually connect to the mind of the animal concerned. That's something I haven't done.

We dowsers have a special ability to do these things, which everybody has. We just work on it a little harder than everybody else. You need to be able to relax. The top athletes call it going "into the zone."

People say, "But I can't dowse. It didn't work for me." I

ask them, "How long did it take you to learn to walk?" First of all, you crawl. Then you pull yourself up on the furniture, then you pull yourself along. How long did that take, about three or four years? And you tell me you couldn't learn to dowse after only five months! Practice, practice, practice! Can anybody dowse? Probably not, because not many people are willing to spend that amount of time working on it.

I was dowsing for probably ten years, dowsing books, asking, "Is this the truth? What percentage of it is the truth?" [I continued] Reading other books. Michael G. Smith's book, *Crystal Power* gave me a jolt in the right direction. I went and built my power rod. I've been doing that for the past 20 years, I suppose.

Also, the best way of learning something is to teach somebody else. So I went along to the Dowsing Society to do a practical evening. We've done all sorts of things, like clearing water. Comparing milk from the supermarket with milk from the farm here. I think one of the most memorable ones, I took photographs of various cars, including the one we had just [bought]. And we dowsed a list of questions. One question was, "Will this car leave us stranded on the side of the road within 150K?" But I got the question wrong because the car didn't leave us stranded on the side of the road only because my son came along and gave us a ride. In other words, the question should have been refined to, "Will this car need a tow truck?" [laughs] Dowsing has a lot of different facets.

Bill stands with a pair of horses at Keeneland in Lexington, Kentucky. Keeneland is an internationally renowned racecourse and a leading Thoroughbred auction house.

About Bill Northern

Bill's globetrotting search for water and his healing of sick horses is a far cry from his early life in the United States where he grew up in Warsaw, a small town in eastern Virginia. In Warsaw, Bill's lifelong love of horses developed. By modern standards, he had a hard childhood. His father, who ran a general store in the town, died when Bill was just seven. Bill's mother, lacking sufficient business acumen to run the store, sold the business.

Life for Bill and his mother was a financial struggle. When he was 12, he began working 30 hours a week in his uncle's restaurant, fitting work around school. Bill busied himself at the restaurant for five years, using the proceeds from some of his labors to get his uncle to buy him a typewriter he used as his ticket to better school marks. "My handwriting was not very good and you got better grades if you typed your assignments," he explains.

The effort paid off as Bill was awarded a scholarship to attend the University of Richmond. But he says he didn't use the time productively. "I ended up spending most of my time playing poker, playing in a band, and shooting on the rifle team. I didn't work."

After another unsuccessful stint at a second university, Bill headed to Washington D.C. where he worked in a hotel and rubbed shoulders with some of the capitol's movers and shakers before returning to Warsaw, where he set up his janitorial supplies business, Wardico.

He was drawn into the world of horse racing and working as a judge at racetracks. He has also owned between 30 and 35 trotters in his time, although he says he only ever owned one he would describe as successful. That was before he discovered dowsing and developed his skills.

Bill ran Wardico for 25 years until he discovered dowsing. He subsequently retired from the business world to concentrate on dowsing. He started to travel half the year to attend horse shows throughout the eastern United States during summer. In 1989, he started to travel to New Zealand to avoid harsh North American winters, although he says it's the warm, friendly people that are the biggest draw for him. He regularly stayed in Rakaia, a town he feels is similar in size to his hometown back in Virginia. He dabbled in real estate in New Zealand but gave up to devote his energies to filling dry wells and horses.

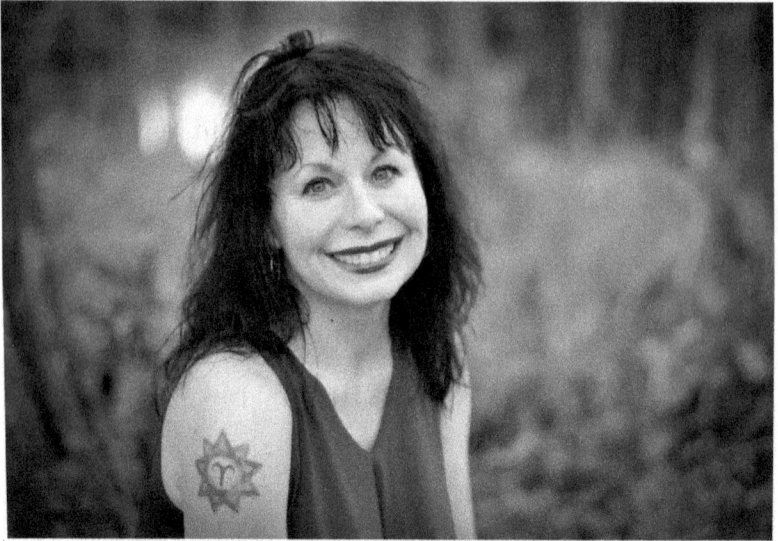

Cesca is pictured on the campus of the University of Louisiana in Lafayette, sitting alongside Cypress Lake.

About Cesca Janece Waterfield

Cesca Janece Waterfield grew up in Alabama and on the Rappahannock River of Virginia like generations of her father's family. She earned an MFA in Creative Writing and an MA in Literature at McNeese State University in Lake Charles, Louisiana. Her reporting has appeared in *the Palm Beach Post, Savannah Morning News, Virginian-Pilot, Free Lance-Star, American Military News,* and more. Her poetry and short fiction have appeared in *The Comstock Review, Scalawag Magazine, Mystery Tribune, Deep South Magazine, LUMINA,* and more. She is the author most recently of *Conspiracy Cherry* (Ludic Arts) and *The Oyster Garden* (Selene Pressworks). She taught college writing from 2014 to 2019 in Louisiana and Wisconsin, and is currently at work on a memoir titled, *Cicada Acre.* Her manuscript, "The

Helicopter War: An Oral History of the Fort Rucker Aviators Class of 1960" is maintained at the United States Army Aviation Museum in Fort Rucker, Alabama.

Honey House Book Hive is named for a century-old cabin on the Rappahannock River that Cesca's parents restored in the 1970s. Within the walls of the old house, they discovered thriving hives of bees and honey. From that day, they referred to the property as "the honey house." When Cesca began working with writers to bring their books to the world, she found inspiration in the unforgettable image of hives flourishing within a formerly abandoned house.

HONEY HOUSE

PRESS + BOOK HIVE

Honey House Press + Book Hive works with writers to develop informal works into books with great readability that maintain the writer's authentic voice.

Everyone has a story. We can help gather and tell your story or the life story of a loved one to reach any audience you want. We will work with you every step of the way, or one step at a time.

www.honeyhousehive.com

247

www.ingramcontent.com/pod-product-compliance
Lightning Source LLC
Chambersburg PA
CBHW062124020426
42335CB00013B/1082